TIME TO ACT

I hear, I forget.
I see, I remember.
I do, I understand.

ANCIENT PROVERB

Affectionately dedicated to all the students, teachers, doctors, lawyers, social workers, caterers, midwives, merchant bankers and many other members of Breadrock Theatre Company, who should share the credit (or blame, depending on your point of view) for pioneering this material.

TIME TO ACT

*Sketches and Guidelines
for Biblical Drama*

by

Paul Burbridge & Murray Watts

HODDER AND STOUGHTON
LONDON   SYDNEY   AUCKLAND   TORONTO

British Library Cataloguing in Publication Data

Burbridge, Paul
  Time to Act.
  1. Christian drama   2. Liturgical drama
  I. Title   II. Watts, Murray
  822'.9'14   PR6052.U/
ISBN 0 340 24699 5

Foreword

These scripts have been much sought after for some time by Christian groups in many parts of the world, and I am delighted that they are now available.

They spring originally from a Christian street-theatre group called Breadrock, and more recently from an off-shoot of that, a professional theatre company, Riding Lights, based on my church – St. Michael-le-Belfrey, York. I have worked with this group for several years, and have consistently witnessed their extraordinary effectiveness in communicating the good news of Jesus Christ. A contemporary version of the medieval mystery plays, they have highlighted some of the original impact of the radical teaching of Jesus, as well as other biblical events and stories – often in the arresting context of humour. I have been with them working on the streets and in prisons, clubs, schools, churches, theatres, television, radio, city-halls – always commanding rapt attention and making considerable impact. It has been my greatest joy and privilege working with them.

God is the God of drama. Not only did the prophets, such as Ezekiel and Agabus, reinforce the thrust of their message in highly dramatic form; but nothing could be greater 'drama' than the incarnation itself, when God became flesh in Jesus Christ. Here is God's supreme communication of himself, and yet the Church has too often dulled this by a profusion of spoken words.

This group, which sensitively, prayerfully and seriously is making highly relevant Christian communication for the latter part of the twentieth century, has both vision and artistic material for which every church should be profoundly thankful.

David Watson

Licences to perform the sketches in this volume

Contents

INTRODUCTION

This book is to encourage you. If you are already involved in creative drama in your church, we want you to explore new avenues, developing material, techniques, and understanding. If you would like to be involved creatively in drama but don't know how, we would like you to have a go. If you have honest doubts about drama, whether it is right or helpful for Christians to occupy themselves with art forms of this kind, then we want to encourage you too. In the latter case, we are anxious to respect doubts but also to allay fears which are sometimes ill-founded. The primary aim of the book is to glorify God by offering back to him gifts he has given to us and to encourage our readers to do the same.

Where did all this start? It started on a beach in North Wales, in a town called Abersoch. If you had looked carefully at this beach in 1956 you could have seen the authors, aged three, pottering backwards and forwards between building sandcastles and attending children's beach services. From that time sprang our friendship but also our sense of debt to the children's mission of that town. We came back seventeen years later, in 1973, to run a mission ourselves – this time to teenagers, and decided to write sketches and perform them as a means of communicating our Christian faith. But it turned out that we couldn't persuade people to come into a church hall, even though it was raining outside, and that we simply had to take our plays onto the streets. Our pulse rates galloping, we set up our ladder and a few props opposite the pub and performed to a hundred of the customers. Hecklers included, it was a resounding success. We felt we had spoken our message with clarity and humour and with some dramatic power. As we look back now to that 'break' with our previous experience of mission work, we feel more enthusiastic about the crowd that gathered than the quality of our early material (and acting). We wanted to go on exploring this means of communication. Instinct and the encouragement of others, not to mention plenty of other people who had experimented in a similar way, told us to go ahead.

Breadrock, an amateur street theatre company, was formed. We enlarged 'bedrock', with its sense of abiding and firm foundation in Christ to include 'bread' as well – the other side of Christ's nature, nourishing as well as supporting us. We've had just about every imaginable variation of the name, including 'deadlock' and 'bedsock', but it has served us well. For five years Breadrock has been the liveliest, the silliest but the most endearing group of Christians either of us have ever worked with: and together we have been into pubs, youth clubs, market squares, churches, beaches, Cheshire Homes, hospitals, foreign language schools, leisure centres, shopping centres, prisons, working men's clubs, school assembly halls. Some of these places have been 'one-off' visits, but others – particularly the open air venues – have become familiar ground.

All the sketches published in the book were written either jointly or individually and with two exceptions were intended for Breadrock. All of these have been proved in performance by Breadrock but we offer them confident that they may inspire you to write better pieces. This book is not just a manual of sketches: we have deliberately concentrated just as much on articles of both practical and theoretical assistance to anyone who wants to experiment for themselves. A book of sketches, pure and simple, would soon get done to death and there would be no resources to renew material and no lessons learnt. We hope very sincerely that the sketches offered here, as well as being useful to perform, will act as pointers, suggestions as to how some of the ideas may be carried out. They are only the 'first word', definitely not the 'last word' in material of this kind. Moreover, it will be clear that some of the articles go beyond the scope of sketch-writing and we would like the book to be an encouragement towards general interest in the arts, and wider exploration of dramatic art in particular.

The kingdom of God is not easily confined to our systems, whether artistic, theological, or materialistic, and it is certainly not possible to encapsulate the greatness of God in a sketch. What it is possible to do is to direct attention, humbly but confidently, to a God who communicates:

The Mighty One, God the Lord,
speaks and summons the earth
from the rising of the sun to its setting.
Out of Zion, the perfection of beauty,
God shines forth.

(Ps. 50)

The wonder of it is that God chooses people to communicate his character and that he does not despise the limitations of our personalities. He does not crush us and mould us into conveyor-belt Christians, but he adorns our lives with laughter, compassion, individuality and different gifts. Therefore, though we know that this book is really conditioned by our personalities, we also believe that God has condescended to communicate something of himself through us and, potentially, through any of our readers.

We owe special thanks to David Watson and all the members of St. Michael-le-Belfrey in York. They have bravely allowed us to make York our home, from September 1977, and even to form a full-time company, Riding Lights Theatre Company, as part of the church's ministry – in mission work, but also in schools, universities and the wider context of professional theatre. We have had so much encouragement and vital material support from St. Michael's that we can only thank God for such a secure home and loving family. It is our hope that St. Michael's special interest in this work will be an incentive and inspiration to many other churches.

Paul Burbridge & Murray Watts.
YORK,
NOVEMBER, 1978.

THE CHURCH AND DRAMA

Many people, not least Christians themselves, are unaware that the roots of the English dramatic tradition lie within the liturgy of the church. Although other influences were brought to bear later, for instance from classical tragedy, the earliest English drama derives from the Latin mass of the middle ages. The simple refrains of the liturgy were elaborated first into dramatic dialogues between the officiating priests and then into playlets on events in the life of Christ. Latin soon gave way to the vernacular and the result of this development was the many different cycles of Mystery Plays, some of which have been revived and are regularly performed today. This close connection between church worship and live theatre has been lost for several centuries,but the time is now ripe for Christians to re-explore the great potential of this relationship.

It is not difficult to see why the dramatic tradition arose out of the worship of the church since all the main services of the church are themselves profoundly 'dramatic'. Celebration of communion is a vivid dramatic memorial of Jesus' last supper with his disciples. Baptism and marriage are both services where outward symbolic action signifies the deeper spiritual reality of the heart. In the main festivals of the church's calendar, too, there are many simple actions, such as the giving of Christmas gifts, which symbolise and commemorate vital spiritual truth. In this way the church has always unconsciously recognised man's need to see outward evidence of – and symbolically to participate in – the work and world of the Spirit.

It is in the context of teaching and preaching that some form of dramatic presentation fits most readily into a modern service of worship. Because of the inevitable spectator element in any dramatic performance, a sketch or dramatic reading in a service is not usually – in a conventional sense – worshipful for the whole congregation (in the way that the singing of a hymn is 'corporate worship'). But a sketch, like a sermon, can *inspire* worship (see 'the Light of the World',

p. 69). Thomas remained a doubter until, on his own terms, he saw the wounds of Jesus, but his instant reaction was to kneel in worship at the feet of his Lord and his God. So, too, the visual is often helpful in focusing people's attention more sharply onto those things about God which demand our worship. Having said all this, the Bible speaks of worship in broader terms than is generally understood. Worship, according to Romans 12 v. 1, involves the offering of our whole bodies and this includes the dedication of our gifts to God. As well as an inspiration to worship, the offering of artistic gifts in church, rightly understood and applied, can be an act of worship in itself.

SOME PRACTICAL GUIDELINES

Forming a Drama Group in a Church

(1) This can often start with as few as two people wanting to do this and receiving the encouragement of their minister. Committed prayer from a very small group can produce openings where there were none before. Many ministers, it should be emphasised, are only too pleased when initiative of this kind is taken.

(2) Once the group is formed, low-key but *good leadership* is essential.

(3) *Pastoral oversight* is a help. Either a minister or an older member of the church, preferably one who has some interest and understanding of drama, should be asked. They can give advice on personal issues, encouragement and perspective. A knowledge of drama is not essential for this role but sympathy and some vision for the work of the group is.

(4) Ideally the group should *meet once a week*, certainly regularly. Half-hearted commitment is worse than useless because it takes a great deal of time and energy to produce good work.

(5) Meetings should have a *clear objective*: e.g. a workshop (see *Glossary*), including physical fitness, improvisations, games of charades, etc., or a talk by a visiting speaker and a discussion, or a visit to a local play production or, most important, rehearsal of material. A leader should not open with 'right, what shall we do?'

(6) The group should work towards a production of some sort as often as possible to *avoid going stale*, always leaving time for experiments and discussion.

Sketches without Writers

Most groups founder through lack of material rather than lack of enthusiasm. The Bible, however, is a store-house of readymade material for those who feel unsure about writing their own.

(1) Some of the most dramatic accounts can be divided up into *a very simple Biblical script*, often making use of a narrator (e.g. Abraham and Isaac, Elijah and the prophets of Baal, the Passion story).

(2) *Mime* is an ideal way of communicating simple stories (see 'The Widow's Mites' p. 48). It is also very close to the roots of drama in history and can move people in a way that the spoken word often fails to do. It can be performed to a background of music or words from the Bible.

(3) *Dance Drama.* This is very akin to mime but often involves the expressiveness of a whole group and may, as with dance, express ideas through symbolic actions. *Warning*: although one of the simplest expedients of the drama group, dance drama is often the hardest to direct, stage and perform well. It can easily become vague and sloppy but, when well done, can be an intensely powerful experience to watch. A good subject, for instance, for dance drama or group mime is psalm 73.

The moral of this section is: read the Bible thoroughly and extensively, not to mention the classics of Christian literature, and do not moan about not having enough material!

Writing Sketches

(1) A group should write its own sketches whenever possible. Many people, who never thought they could, can write this sort of material and learn to do it well. The main thing is to break the ice, *have a go* and learn by experience. Drama groups can try out new sketches without necessarily letting them see the light of day. Personal feelings are obviously involved but the leader should have the respect of the group and be able to say 'this is not good enough yet'.

(2) *Do not write by committee.* Ideas may come out of a group and mimes can often arise through group improvisations, but a good script is usually the work of one or two people. Partnership is often good for comedy but it needs a good relationship as each party may have to back down over a particular line or idea.

(3) Study *the context and the environment* for the performance.

(a) Context: does it stand on its own? (e.g. street theatre). Is it part of a worship service? In this case it is vital to 'tone in' the sketch with the whole proceedings – damage may be caused to the reception of your work by insensitively 'jarring the atmosphere' of a service. Many people have very strong feelings about what is appropriate in church.

(b) Environment: What are your acoustics and sight-lines like? Do you need a sketch that concentrates on one small, raised area? Church buildings are invariably problematic for any live drama. Pillars galore, high-backed pews and large pulpits usually ensure that some proportion of the congregation will not be able to see everything. Acoustically, churches are often poor as well. You may need to write material around the use of a P.A. system (perhaps by using a narrator and mime technique). Good sketches are not concerned merely with ideas, but with the practicalities of any dramatic performance.

(4) *Decide on your subject.* The ideal is to decide on the subject after context and environment have been taken into account, but a speaker may have already made the decision. If so, work in close cooperation with him whenever possible. Try to persuade him not to 'kill dead' your sketch by failing to make any reference to it at all, in return for faithfully setting up the subject of his talk as best you can.

(5) *Pray.* It is vital to seek God's guidance in understanding the point you are trying to put over. If *you* do not understand it, you are unlikely to help others to do so. *Warning*: never refuse to accept criticism of a sketch because you have 'prayed about it' or 'been led to it'. Sketch writing is like any other human activity – subject to human mistakes. God guides faithfully and helps us to develop our gifts. Part of this development may be accepting criticism and learning from our mistakes.

(6) *Length.* Sketches are almost always too long rather than too short. There is no rule for length but it is good to be adept at the three-minute sketch because this disciplines you to clarity and simplicity. Five to ten minutes are for more meaty ideas and fifteen to twenty minutes is generally the outside length without trying to write a short play. It is vital never to write more material (in consideration of your available writing and acting talents) than can fully hold an audience's attention.

(7) A good sketch has several and sometimes all of the following qualities:

Pace. This means fast exits and entrances, not giving characters too much to say, pithy interchange of dialogue (pace is very important in street theatre).

Simplicity. This usually means one point, perhaps looked at in different ways and dramatically summed up at the end.

Humour. This builds up a warm relationship with an audience as well as sharpening their concentration. It can break down barriers, teach without threatening and help us not to take ourselves too seriously (it usually causes offence only to those who yield to that temptation). Humour, however, is not just a tool but has tremendous value for its own sake as a gift from God (see article p. 120).

Shock or Surprise Value. The sketch writer may want to cut laughter short suddenly to impress the seriousness of a particular point. A sudden change of tempo, a new character, a verse of scripture, a dramatic stylised movement in mime will add vividness to a piece and prevent it from boring the audience, because they feel they know 'what is going to happen next'. A good sketch will often be full of surprises.

Dramatic Finish. A sketch that tails off loses at least fifty per cent of its force. Most people remember a sketch best when it has finished powerfully and well. A dramatic finish is not necessarily a 'finish with a punch' but maybe a gentle and sustained 'fade off' with characters walking off slowly or the lights being gradually dimmed (if available). The aspect of endings to remember is control – it should be apparent that the piece is meant to end this way, not because somebody has dried. Alternatively, a sudden freeze can be very effective or a pithy summing up of the point by the narrator. (Nobody should move carelessly at the end of a sketch and several seconds of silence at least should be given to the audience when it has finished, before the actors move.) It goes without saying that a sketch can be completely serious without 'humorous touches' but in such cases final effectiveness is heavily dependent on observing control throughout and a dramatic finish.

Music

Music can be a very useful backup for drama if used in a sensitive way. Beware of sentimentalising by the over-use of romantic 'slush' or heavy dramatic discords, unless you want to turn the action into melodrama! (Try this exercise for fun: when you next watch a Western, or an American TV programme, listen especially to the music – when and why it is used, and whether to good or bad effect.) The main thing to remember is to be simple and definite, and to tend towards underplaying rather than overplaying.

Where to use music:

(1) *To introduce and end a sketch*: this sets the mood or winds up the sketch and need only be about ten seconds long.

(2) *Dramatic moments*: often silence will be the best thing, but sometimes music will be appropriate, and will enhance the effect – for example, humming a simple melody to the accompaniment of the guitar when Christ is taken off the cross in 'The Light of the World'. (See page 72.)

(3) *Mime*: it is probably easiest to play the piano for mime, but guitar and a solo instrument could also be effective.

(a) choosing well-known tunes to suit the action – e.g. 'If I were a rich man' for the rich Pharisee putting money in the treasury, in 'The Widow's Mites'. (See page 48.)

Be careful to link different tunes in the same sketch, either by the key, or a repeated phrase, etc. – the music throughout should flow, and the actors should not be left with unexpected silences!

(b) mood music – improvising themes to suit the general action of the mime. Some hints – for sad parts, use minor keys and slow-moving chords; for happy parts use brisk melodies in the middle/upper register in either major or minor keys.

NB There is no need for complex chord changes – simple is effective. In all musical mime, the music must be tailored carefully to the action. For the actors' sake, work out definite cues for different stages of the action.

(4) *Incidental music for street theatre or an indoor revue*: the intervals between sketches when the actors are rushing around getting changed for the next sketch can be covered

by improvised music, reflecting the mood at the end of the last sketch and moving into the beginning of the next.

Instruments:

The piano is probably the most useful instrument – but has somewhat limited use in street theatre! Many effects can be produced on it – experiment with new sounds.

Next to the piano, the guitar is the most versatile. Again, many sound effects can be produced – heart beats, drums, driving rhythms, 'eerie' sound produced by plucking a high note and then stretching it with the left hand finger.

Other useful instruments are the kazoo, jingle bells and tin whistle – all very cheap – and solo instruments such as the violin or flute. Trumpets tend to be too loud, unless that is the effect wanted.

In general, with imagination, flair and sensitivity, the kind of sketches in this book can all be enlivened by touches of musical colour, appropriate to their various contexts.

Rehearsing Sketches

(1) *Director*. There must be one for a particular rehearsal (who it is may vary). *Warning*: this is a difficult job and it is no good having somebody with insufficient control over the group.

(2) *Actors*. Don't shout out suggestions, argue with the director or fool about. Follow the director's instructions with the minimum of fuss. Make (sensible) suggestions to the director if he wants them.

(3) *Spectators*. These sometimes mysteriously congregate during the rehearsals with or without the approval of the group (particularly if you rehearse in a church hall). Aim for privacy in rehearsal. Draw curtains if necessary. Any spectators you want there should be kept to a minimum and should observe exactly the same discipline as the actors. Silence is the rule for the rehearsal room and it must be enforced courteously by the director with the maximum co-operation from all present. More energy is lost and more tempers frayed by people talking and fooling during rehearsals than by most other aspects of the work of a drama group.

(4) *Running the Rehearsal*. Directors are advised to give a good warm-up to begin with to avoid muscles being strained and to help people let off steam. If actors are visibly chafing during a lengthy piece of work with one person, it may be an idea to stop the rehearsal and play a quick game to keep everybody on their toes. Those who are not involved in a particular sketch should learn what they can from watching, read up a book (e.g. on mime), make props or do something useful. Reading books, it should be emphasised, is important for anyone leading a drama group: there are many available on improvisation, fitness, mime and most aspects of drama. (see Bibliography p. 128)

Presenting Sketches

(1) *Compère*. Sometimes a *brief*, relaxed introduction to a sketch may help to avoid bad 'toning in' with a service. Do not have somebody unconnected with the group to do this, if possible, and discourage lengthy discourses at the opening and close of any longer show you do. It is better to say a little at the beginning of a performance and to avoid saying anything at the end (unless there is a talk planned to follow).

(2) *Start on time*. It is better that a late audience should delay you than a late performance should delay (and frustrate) them. Bad timing at the beginning can put a sketch off balance. If you are part of a service be slick about your cues and finish in the time allotted to you.

(3) *Concentrate your action*. Never confuse an audience with too many actors in too many places. Don't allow anybody playing a walk-on part to 'upstage' your main character unless you specifically want this. The test of a good actor is often his ability to play a small part with restraint.

(4) *Diction*. This is vitally important, especially so in buildings not designed for drama. Rehearsals should involve exercises to improve diction and voice projection (see *Bibliography*).

(5) *Dress*. The east end of many church buildings is often very visually confusing as a background to a sketch, in which case stylised costume can help to make the characters stand out. Plain colours or black may be the best. Since most presentations within services have to be kept short,

elaborate costumes and props are unnecessary. The temptation to think that the Bible can only be dramatised properly in full Biblical dress, a profusion of robes etc., should also be resisted. Your acting makes a character real, not your costume, and modern dress nearly always adds a freshness and relevance to Biblical material. In general, it is better to costume a sketch very well or very plainly (sometimes, as in street theatre, motley and outlandish costumes can be very good fun but such an effect should be through design rather than ineptitude). Careful attention to design of costumes can mean a wider circle involved in the work of the drama group.

(6) *Set.* This is not usually practicable except for longer pieces. Simple, stylised props are often best. Sometimes a drape can help to simplify a confusing background (particularly in the case of mime). An active drama group should consider some kind of easily portable flats to create their own set if they want it; in addition to this, stage blocks which can be swiftly erected in a chancel area or used to give adequate sightlines in a hall without a stage can be very valuable equipment for a group performing regularly.

(7) *Stage Management.* An efficient stage manager to organise the wardrobe, the setting and striking of props and the overall smooth running of the performance is a priority. In a more sophisticated setting, the S.M. will also give cues to sound and lighting operators, or if stage hands are available, may operate the technical aspects of the production.

Points for Careful Consideration

(1) *Publicity.* Good publicity for a dramatic performance, a guest service or any event involving a drama group is essential. The publicity for many Christian activities is lamentable. Sloppy posters with poor colour combinations, confusing typography and patronising use of jargon ('come and join us in a time of sharing', 'do pop round for coffee and just a chat', 'we'll be having a super time. See you there!') effectively wipe out the sensitive half of a potential audience. Those who have gifts in design should use them to the full to raise the standard of Christian publicity.

Choosing of titles for events is always difficult, avoiding both cliché and obscurity. Be honest in your advertising, but confident. Above all, be attractive and think your way into the minds of people who are likely to be put off by the conventional image of the church. Don't give too much information – just what is necessary. Intrigue people. Use humorous drawings or good, stylish design. Don't try and convey all your message, and be careful to avoid sentimentalism and over-intensity. It is good to get posters, especially if they are well conceived, into places where the widest and least predictable audiences can be attracted.

As well as posters and handouts, publicity can mean keeping local radio informed (best of all through a personal contact), publicity stunts in the streets, accompanied by handbills, and newspaper advertising. Too many groups think that prayer unaccompanied by initiative and hard work, will provide a good audience. To re-work a rather well-worn phrase: 'why should the devil have all the good publicity?'

(2) *Etiquette*. Inexperience in simple etiquette can cause friction between Christians involved in drama. *Never* tape anybody's material, no matter how officially you may have been appointed, without asking their prior permission. Likewise, never reproduce, print out or perform any material without authorisation from the owner of the copyright. In cases of unpublished material, always find out who wrote it and consult them before using it in any form.

Conclusion

Forming a drama group within the context of a church fellowship needs great commitment and vision to be successful. It needs an awareness of having a real ministry through drama, both in the group itself and in the congregation who will listen to God's word speaking through them. The group will need deep relationships together for the good of their acting and for the sake of discerning spiritually the up-to-date needs of their church. Church members of all ages should be involved. This is a serious and significant ministry within the life of the church, but its effectiveness is hindered if it is seen only as something occasional and 'nice' for young people, or worse, as being the special province of small Sunday school children at Christmas time. Children should be encouraged, but they are best encouraged by learning from adults doing the same thing.

A committed drama group that is prayerful and imaginative about its work can gradually begin to influence church 'culture'. The art-forms that are normally prevalent in church worship provide an alarming culture-shock to anyone coming in from the outside. Christians need not be afraid to learn from the best of the society in which they live, so that what happens artistically *inside* the church is relevant and is, in turn, able to make a positive contribution by enriching the world around it.

Many people cannot be directly involved in this ministry, but by their attitude, prayers and patronage they can profoundly encourage those who are. Groups that operate full time need money, as any missionaries do, in order to pursue their work; every kind of group, both amateur and professional, needs prayer. Christian parents have a particular responsibility to their children. Education today has an emphasis on drama, movement, self-expression. This can be used rightly: Christian parents should help their families to develop a critical intellect. Both minds and bodies should be trained from the earliest. Children have a natural flair for drama up to the age of about eleven or more and their gifts should be developed. The church of tomorrow needs communicators.

SKETCHES FOR CHURCH SERVICES

The Parable of the Talents

NARRATOR ONE NARRATOR TWO DRACULA FRED, a hard-working gardener TED, an astute salesman JULIAN POTTER-TON-BROWN, a self-preoccupied fop THE MASTER, a stern but kindly landlord

Read the introduction to THE HOUSE ON THE ROCK (p. 55). Costumes for the actors in the mime should be typical of their characters. Unlike the other two narrator sketches THE PARABLE OF THE TALENTS is most reliably performed indoors (the text is more elaborate) but feel free to prove us wrong.

ONE: Matthew
TWO: Twenty five
ONE: Verse
TWO: Fourteen.
ONE: The parable of THE TALONS!
    (*Dramatic music. Enter* DRACULA *in evening dress, with swirling cape and long talons on his fingers. He threatens the audience melodramatically. The two* NARRATORS *confer.*)
TWO: (*Explaining to the audience*). I'm sorry, apparently what we've got here is the parable of the *talents.*
    (*Exit* DRACULA, *mortified that his moment of glory has been cut short. One of the* NARRATORS *can improvise, using the ordinary name of the actor: 'it was a nice idea, Geoffrey, but . . .'*)
ONE: Begin again.
TWO: Matthew
ONE: Twenty five
TWO: Verse

ONE: Fourteen.

TWO: Jesus told a story

ONE: About

TWO: A man

ONE: Who had

TWO: Three servants – for the sake of argument:

ONE: Fred,
(*Pause while* FRED *enters and takes up position.*)

TWO: Ted,
(*Pause while* TED *enters and takes up position.*)

ONE: And Julian Potterton-Brown.
(*Longer pause while* JULIAN POTTERTON-BROWN *makes a fastidious entrance.*)

TWO: Now Ted was smarter than Fred.

ONE: But Fred was bigger than Ted.

TWO: Ted had a head to earn him his bread

ONE: Which cannot be said for Fred.

TWO: But Fred often said:

ONE: 'I don't 'ave Ted's 'ead

TWO: I manage wiv muscles instead.'

ONE: Now Julian Potterton-Brown

TWO: Was the odd one out.

ONE: But this didn't deter him – after all:

TWO: 'I'm frightfully well-bred,' he said.

ONE: 'I'm greasier than Ted,' he said.

TWO: 'I'm lazier than Fred,' he said.

ONE: 'And I don't rhyme with either of them, the creeps.'

TWO: One day their employer summoned them to his office.
(*Enter* THE MASTER. *He sits at a desk.*)

ONE: Knock, knock.

TWO: 'Come in.

ONE: Now listen you three.

TWO: Fred, Ted and Julian whateveryourname is.'

ONE: (JULIAN *prompting him*). 'Potterton-Brown.'

TWO: 'Granted.'

ONE: 'Before I go away on my journey

TWO: I wish to give you each some money to look after.

ONE: Form a queue, form a queue.
(JULIAN *makes sure he gets to the front, but* THE MASTER *bypasses him and goes straight to* FRED *at the end of the queue.*)

TWO: Five talents for you.

ONE: Two talents for you. (*Given to* TED.)

TWO: And one talent for you.' (JULIAN *looks at it disparagingly.*)

ONE: So he waved goodbye.

TWO: He took his toothbrush.

ONE: Took his hat.

TWO: Took his coat.

ONE: Took his leave

TWO: And left.
(*Exit* MASTER.)

ONE: Now Fred had two thousand five hundred pounds.

TWO: Ted had one thousand pounds.

ONE: Julian had five hundred pounds.

TWO: But what were they going to do with it?

ONE: Fred had a flair for gardening and fancied growing some vegetables.

TWO: Ted had a flair for marketing and fancied his chances in business.

ONE: Julian had flairs and fancied himself.

TWO: Fred rolled up his sleeves

ONE: Grabbed his money

TWO: And blew the whole lot on a spade

ONE: A garden shed

TWO: A plot o' land

ONE: A bag o' bulbs

TWO: An 'osepipe

ONE: And a pair of wellies.

TWO: And got stuck in.

ONE: The wellies.

TWO: Wellies not often that you . . .

ONE: Oh shut up.

TWO: Sorry. Ted surveyed the market very carefully.

ONE: Bided his time

TWO: Picked his moment

ONE: Got his wallet

TWO: Laid all 'his money on twenty

ONE: Second 'and camels.

TWO: Julian was sensible

ONE: Was wise

TWO: Was cautious

ONE: He considered the problems

TWO: The pitfalls

ONE: The dangers that lay ahead

TWO: The risk of losing everything.

ONE: And so Julian used his intelligence

TWO: He thought

ONE: He planned

TWO: He schemed

ONE: He did

TWO: Nothing.

ONE: Nothing.

TWO: But he was jolly careful with his money.

ONE: He wrapped it up in a silk handkerchief

TWO: On a velvet cushion

ONE: In a little box

TWO: And hid it under the floorboards.

ONE: And then:

TWO: A few years later:

ONE: Knock, knock.

TWO: Who's there?

ONE: Who do you think?

TWO: The master!

ONE: (*Gasping*). The master!

TWO: Quick, quick, form a queue, form a queue

ONE: Same to you

TWO: Shut up

ONE: Shut up yourself.

TWO: Sssssh!

ONE: Ssh!

> (*During this kerfuffle* JULIAN *has made sure, in contrast to the previous line-up, that he is at the back. The* MASTER *returns.*)

TWO: And the master called each man to account for the money he had entrusted to him.

ONE: 'Who's first?'
(FRED, *finding himself at the front of the queue, reluctantly comes forward.*)

TWO: 'Well, it's not as much as I'd hoped master, cabbages got frostbitten last year . . .'

ONE: 'Never mind that – well done, good and faithful servant!

TWO: You have doubled the money I gave you.

ONE: Enter into the joy of your Lord.

TWO: Next.'
(TED *comes forward.*)

ONE: 'Yeah – well – er, second 'and camels – sold a few, bought a few, crashed a few – but you can't win 'em all, so 'ere you are.'

TWO: 'Well done, good and faithful servant!

ONE: You too have doubled the money I gave you.

TWO: Enter into the joy of your Lord.

ONE: Next.'
(JULIAN *takes out a prepared speech.*)

TWO: (*Loud cough*)

ONE: (*Sound of clearing throat*)
(JULIAN *applies a throat spray.*)

TWO: 'Master!

ONE: My Lord!

TWO: (*Ingratiatingly*). Master . . .

ONE: Knowing you to be a hard man, etc., etc.

TWO: Blah blah blah, reaping where you did not sow

ONE: Blah blah blah, gathering where you did not winnow

TWO: Ploughing where you did not . . .
(*Fighting for words*) plough, and so on . .

ONE: And so forth . . .

TWO: I was afraid and hid the money.

ONE: I remain your obedient servant, Julian

Pott—'
(*His speech is cut short by the* MASTER
*snatching the paper from his hand and
tearing it up. If the paper is mimed, one
of the narrators should make a suitable
ripping noise.*)

TWO: 'You did nothing!

ONE: You're all words.

TWO: You're all talk.

ONE: All that I gave you has not grown one
inch!

TWO: Take away the talent and give it to the
man who has ten.

ONE: And take this wicked servant and cast
him into outer darkness.
(JULIAN *is dragged off stage by invisible
forces. The* MASTER *turns, as if to address
the audience:*)

TWO: Don't be deceived.

ONE: Put everything that God has given you
to good use.

TWO: For one day you will have to give an
account of your life

ONE: To him.'

One for Me and None for You

DIVES, a rich man   LAZARUS, a pauper   CHANTING VOICE
HUSBAND   WIFE   T.V. ANNOUNCER

Perhaps the hardest thing of all in producing a sketch for a Christian context is 'getting through' to Christians who have heard Bible stories, and sermons expounding them, so often. This sketch was written to bring the message of Dives and Lazarus close to home. For those writing new material, there is considerable scope for sketches treating subjects like lifestyle, stewardship, prejudice, political exploitation and many other subjects, all of which can be found in the writings of the prophets but need fresh examination for today.

The stage setting requires a table with two chairs and, nearby, a television set angled to face the the audience as well as the characters. The television set is a handy prop which can be made out of an old T.V., hollowed out for an actor to sit with his head looking out of the screen. The piece begins with a dumbshow as follows: DIVES *enters, wearing a purple robe, sits at the table and begins to dine sumptuously. As he says grace and continues in prayer briefly,* LAZARUS *enters in rags and crawls beneath his table. Despite his pleas, he receives nothing and eventually dies. Still ignoring* LAZARUS, DIVES *himself dies, choking to death on his food and offering up desperate prayers as he breathes his last. While this has been continuing, a chant is heard in the background:*

> VOICE: One for me and none for you,
> 'n' two for me and two for me,
> 'n' three for me and none for you,
> 'n' four for me and more for me,
> 'n' five for me and less for you,
> 'n' one for you (DIVES *drops a crumb*)
> and twelve for me,
> 'n' good for me and bad for you,
> 'n' fat for me and thin for you,
> 'n' bully for me and shucks to you.
> (LAZARUS *dies.*)

(*The chant starts again, but finishes abruptly as* DIVES *dies. Exeunt. Enter* HUSBAND *and* WIFE, *who sit down to supper. The* ANNOUNCER *should be already in position, but preferably concealed behind doors in front of the screen or sitting away from the immediate area of the audience's attention.*)

WIFE: Supper's all ready, darling. How was the service tonight?

HUSBAND: Oh, it went pretty well. Pretty full. Shall we say grace? (*They pray silently.*)

WIFE: Good sermon?

HUSBAND: Yes, not bad. It was based on that rather strange story about Dives and Lazarus.

WIFE: Oh, yes. (*Eating*). A rather melodramatic one, if I remember rightly.

HUSBAND: Well, parables have to exaggerate things in order to bring out the point. They wouldn't be parables if they didn't. Mind you, they're very telling little stories, some of them.

WIFE: Yes, and the drama group really do bring the Bible alive, don't they? I think I might find the Bible a little boring without the parables.

HUSBAND: But you still have to make allowances for the fact that they are all speaking about Palestine in the first century. That's the problem. I mean, we don't have starving beggars full of sores dumped on our doorstep with the milk every morning, do we? (*They smile at one another.*)

WIFE: Oh, this came through the letterbox while you were out at church. (*She hands him an envelope.*) I think it's another of those Oxfam things.

HUSBAND: That's the third one this week! We'd better send something off to them before they go sending us more envelopes.

WIFE: Especially after that sermon.

HUSBAND: Yes. Can you put a little in from the housekeeping this week?

WIFE: Well, not very easily. Roy and Jane are coming to dinner tomorrow and I haven't bought the food yet. We can hardly invite them round to a fast!

HUSBAND: Surely you could manage a pound or fifty 'p'. That's all that's necessary really, because they're covering the whole of England and Wales. Not that there's any knowing where the money actually goes, though.
(*They freeze whenever the voice chants:*)

VOICE: One for me and none for you.

WIFE: But the cream alone will cost that.

VOICE: Two for me and none for you.

HUSBAND: Well, it's no good looking at me, we've worked everything out this month already. Especially if we're going to get a decent holiday this year.

VOICE: Three for me and none for you.

WIFE: All right, I'll do it then. But don't expect any wine with the meal.

HUSBAND: But you know I'm already buying the drinks, so what are you worrying about? Put in fifty 'p'. Every little helps, doesn't it?

VOICE: One for you and twelve for me.

WIFE: But it's so cold just sending money in an envelope.

HUSBAND: Be a lot easier if there was a starving beggar on the doorstep. (*Looking at his watch.*) I wonder what's on the box tonight? (*He switches it on.*)

ANNOUNCER: The urgency of the nationwide Oxfam appeal this week has been intensified by the terrible coincidence of two major catastrophes – one in Southern India, where thousands have died and thousands more made homeless by a giant tidal wave which has devastated a whole district. Also, in Peru yesterday, an earthquake struck the capital, Lima, and many square miles of the surrounding countryside. The exact extent of the suffering is not yet clear, say relief workers, but the death toll is already heavy. The governments of both countries have made urgent appeals for help. Many tons of medical supplies, blankets and tents are needed for the sick and homeless. Oxfam say that they are stepping up their campaign to raise funds to cope with what, in India, is said to be the worst ever destruction of farmlands, villages and human life at one time. Please give generously and send money to this address . . .

HUSBAND: Isn't that tragic. (*He goes to switch off.*)

ANNOUNCER: Don't switch off! Sit down and listen to me! (*The* HUSBAND *is nonplussed. He stands where he is.*) This situation is desperate. Could you survive on fifty 'p'? Could you live on half a bowl of rice every three days? They can't eat sympathy, you know. People are dying for lack of food, and there you sit in the West, where your biggest problem is obesity! Listen to me, please, please, share what you have . . . tonight. Don't just switch off!! (*The* HUSBAND *moves embarrassedly to the T.V.*) I'll come and show you if you like . . .

(*The* HUSBAND *switches off the television.*)

HUSBAND: I don't know what to do. It's . . . so embarrassing, that kind of thing.

WIFE: I know.

(*They continue to eat. The* ANNOUNCER *bursts into the room, supporting* LAZARUS *on his shoulder. He lets him down onto the floor, in front of the table. He stands back helplessly as the chant and the end of the dumbshow is repeated: the*

HUSBAND *and* WIFE *go on eating,
oblivious to the silent pleas of the dying*
LAZARUS. *He stretches out for non-
existent scraps, craves for something to
drink, but falls to the ground in slow
motion as the chant finishes. The*
HUSBAND *and* WIFE, *still eating, freeze.)*

Importunity Knocks

NARRATOR MAN, intellectually confused JUDGE, self-centred and embittered WIDOW, a persistent old bag JEREMY, a tired neighbour COLIN, a hearty friend FATHER SON

This sequence is designed as a lengthy illustrative digression interrupting a sermon about the gospel or about receiving the Holy Spirit or about prayer. It can be performed on its own with a short improvised introduction by the NARRATOR *on any of these subjects, but it is primarily intended for indoor performance.*

The stage setting can be simple, but a door and some kind of mattress or bedding will be needed for the second scene. As the speaker is in full flight, at a pre-arranged signal, the MAN *wanders up to the pulpit or onto the stage.*

> MAN: 'Scuse me. 'Scuse me. Sorry, David.
> Hullo. Could I . . . ? Sorry, could I get
> a word in here, please? Just for a minute
> or two, if you wouldn't mind. You
> don't? Good, fine. Well, let's just pause
> for a moment or two here. You see,
> there's no way round it, frankly. I mean,
> when you start talking that kind of
> language I can't relate to it all. Okay?
> In what sense is it meaningful that I – a
> man – can talk to God – a god. *The
> God.* Not so much *the God* as GOD.
> Vastness. Sublime perfection. The . . .
> (*makes a hopeless gesture towards
> infinity*) . . . you know, you just run out
> of words. How can you begin to ask
> God for anything? You talk so glibly
> about asking God for the Holy Spirit!!
> I mean . . . (*sighs*) . . . it's completely
> beyond my ken. To me this is *non –
> sense.* God isn't at my beck and call,

you know, I can't go round asking God
for things . . . Frankly, if I can do
anything at all, I can only contemplate
the tiniest bit . . . (*Enter* NARRATOR).

NARRATOR: Excuse me, is this going to be a long
speech? I mean, are we going to be
sitting around here all night just
listening to you expounding your
personal theories?

MAN: (*Defensively*). No, no, no, I'm not
forcing anybody to . . .

NARRATOR: I mean, *love* to hear whatever it is that
you've got to say but, er, some of us
are finding it just a teensy weensy bit
boring. I'm afraid.

MAN: Oh.

NARRATOR: Now correct me if I'm wrong, but
you're really talking about prayer,
right?

MAN: (*Re-starting his speech*). Prayer. Yes,
that's it! That's the whole problem. How
can one begin to come into
conversational contact with . . . with the
Divine, Essence, Quintessence, call it
what you will, the Transcendent—

NARRATOR: (*Brusquely*). Right. Prayer. Well, you
take a seat – there's one down there in
the front row – and let's get our feet on
some more solid ground, shall we? See
what the Bible *actually says*. Okay?

MAN: The Bible. Well there you go dragging
a whole hornets' nest of problems into—

NARRATOR: Fine, take a seat.

MAN: I'll take one, but can you honestly
expect that—

NARRATOR: Well, let's try. Now, take three simple
pictures which Jesus gave . . .
(*The* MAN *sits down*.)

MAN: Go ahead. Take as many as you like.

NARRATOR: (*Wearily*). Thank you. I will. Now—

MAN: Whatever turns you on. Don't mind me,
I'm only—

NARRATOR: Right, thank you, we won't. As I said, take three simple pictures.

MAN: I'll just shut up. You carry on.

NARRATOR: THANK YOU. (*Silence. The* NARRATOR *looks suspiciously in the direction of the* MAN. *Pause.*) Picture number one: a judge.

(*The* JUDGE *enters and sits at his desk.*) An arrogant so-and-so if ever there was one. He feared neither God nor man (*pause.*) Only his wife. (*The* JUDGE *looks over his shoulder, terrified*). But that's another story. He was the sort of man who treated everybody like the ash on the end of his cigar . . . to be discarded after use. And: a widow.

(*The* WIDOW *enters.*) Oppressed, poor, with no one to defend her against a malicious opponent.

WIDOW: I've got no one to defend me against a malicious opponent. D'yer hear? (*Silence*). I *said*, I've got no one to defend me against a—

JUDGE: Yes, I can hear thank you, Good day.

WIDOW: What are you going to do about it, then?

(*The* JUDGE *reads his newspaper.*) Look at yer. Sat there, day after day, smokin' yer head 'orf. Bet yer not even sober 'arf the time. Well, I'm not goin' till you done somethin' about it. You're the judge and I'm goin' to 'ave justice!! (*She hits the newspaper with her brolly.*) LEGAL AID!! Ever 'eard of it? That's what I want, Legal Aid.

JUDGE: I'm well acquainted with the legal aid system, madam. Thank you.

WIDOW: I've got things to do.

(*She sits down and takes out her knitting.*)

JUDGE: And so, fortunately madam, have I.

WIDOW: I don't care 'ow long I wait, I'm not goin' till I got a settlement. (*Pause*)

Knit one, pearl one, knit one, pearl one, knit—

JUDGE: Oh-for-crying-out-loud!

WIDOW: (*Obligingly*). All right. KNIT ONE, PEARL ONE, KNIT ONE, PEARL ONE!!

JUDGE: (*In an apopleptic frenzy*). MADAM!! (*Silence*) You'll be the death of me. If you promise ... to *go* ... to leave me alone ... and never, ever, ever come back ... I will give you whatever settlement you require.

(*The* JUDGE *and the* WIDOW *freeze.*)

NARRATOR: Jesus said: 'If that corrupt Judge gave that woman what she wanted, simply because she went on and on and on at him, don't you think that *God* will judge in favour of his own people, who cry to him day and night for help. Will he be slow to help them? I tell you, of course he will judge in their favour and do it quickly.

(*Exeunt* JUDGE *and* WIDOW.)

Picture number two: the time is now 11 p.m.

(*Enter* JEREMY *in nightshirt.*)

A man prepares for bed. (*The following actions can be mimed.*) He washes his face, brushes his teeth, files his nails (*for the last action he goes to an imaginary filing cabinet and looks for the correct folder*) ... under N. At this moment there is a knock at the door (*knocking*). It is a friend.

COLIN: (*Speaking from behind the door*). You haven't got two p. for the coin box, have you?

(JEREMY *opens the door.*)

Sorry. Got to ring the mother you see. (JEREMY *patiently rummages through a wallet to find the coin.*) Thanks, thanks awfully. Bye. (*Exit*)

NARRATOR: Silence descends upon the house. The family are asleep. The man turns out the light.
(JEREMY *is tucked up in bed. Pause. Knocking.*)

COLIN: Jeremy – sorry. (JEREMY *gets up and opens the door.*) Did I get you up? Look, could you make it ten p. actually? Mother's going on a bit, you know. Thanks so much. Decent.
(JEREMY *rummages through his wallet a little less patiently.*)

JEREMY: That's okay. Sure there's nothing else I can do for you? Write you a cheque or something?

COLIN: No, no, no, no, those don't go in the box. Bye then. Sleep well. (*Exit*)

NARRATOR: (*Suddenly breaking into a German accent**). Observe how, at last, zis patient little fellow takes his vell-earned beauty sleep. (JEREMY *stubs his toe and cries out.*) Oh dear, see how tired he iss becoming. (JEREMY *collapses into bed.* NARRATOR *resumes normal voice.*) It is now 12 p.m.
(*Knocking*)

COLIN: Sorry. Hello. (*More knocking*). Jeremy, Colin here. Sorry. Got any bread in? Just had some rather unexpected visitors and – whaddyer know? bread.

JEREMY: (*Without moving from bed*). Bread. He's got no bread. (*He sobs.*)

COLIN: You asleep?

JEREMY: Yup. I'm sleeping. *Go away!*

COLIN: I just want some bread, that's all. If it isn't any bother. Just a loaf or two. Three if you've got them. But if you haven't, not to worry. Two would be fine. (*Pause*) Three would be ideal. But not to worry specially. (*Pause*) Tin of sardines would be out of this world.

(JEREMY *shrieks, leaps out of bed,*
unlocks the door and hurls three loaves
of bread at COLIN.)

COLIN: Thanks so much. It's quite all right
about the sardines. (JEREMY *slams the*
door, bolts it and barricades it with his
bed.) Sleep well. (*Freeze*)

NARRATOR: Jesus said: 'I tell you, even if this man
will not get up and give him the bread
because he is his friend, yet he will get
up and give him everything he needs
because he is not ashamed to keep on
asking.'
(*Exeunt* JEREMY *and* COLIN)
Third picture: imagine an ordinary
father with his son. Any father – any
one of you.
(*Enter* FATHER *and* SON (*the* SON *can be*
an adult actor dressed as a schoolboy).
They mime to the narration.)
Now if your son came to you one
morning and said: 'Dad, can I have an
egg for breakfast?', would you give him
a scorpion? (FATHER *suddenly produces*
rubber scorpion. SON *leaps back in*
horror.) I doubt it. Or if he came to you
and said: 'Dad, can I have a fish?',
would you give him a snake? (FATHER
offers him a snake). Of course not. So,
if you who are human, fallible and
sometimes selfish and irritable know
how to give good things to your children,
how much more will God, our father in
heaven, give the Holy Spirit to those
who ask him? (*The* FATHER *acts out a*
true father's relationship with his SON,
producing imaginary hoards of presents.
The SON *is delighted. The* NARRATOR
beckons up the MAN *from the front row.*)
You see, coming to God is as simple as
this: (*The verses are made into a simple*
mimed routine by the FATHER *and the*

SON.) Ask and you shall receive. Seek and you shall find. Knock and the door shall be opened for you. (*The* NARRATOR *invites the* MAN *to join in.*) Go on, you try it.

MAN: This isn't really my scene, you know, amateur dramatics and all that, but . . . if you think it will help . . .
(*He joins in as the mime is repeated. As this happens, all four actors on stage repeat the verses.*)

ALL: Ask and you shall receive. Seek and you shall find. Knock and the door shall be opened for you. (*The last move is for the* MAN *to walk through the imaginary door. He stops, turns and smiles.*)

* Optional reference to a contemporary advert. Other equivalents may be found.

The Appointment

SECRETARY   BUSINESSMAN   JESUS

This is a very simple sketch, based on the encounter between Jesus and the Rich Young Ruler. The character of the BUSINESSMAN *is not identical to that of his Biblical counterpart but the challenge to him is the same. 'Up-dating' stories is simple to do and can be very necessary for church audiences over-familiar with the text (see also ONE FOR ME AND NONE FOR YOU p. 30) – it can also be a revelation, despite apparent incongruity, to see Jesus speaking in a familiar twentieth-century situation. It should also be said that a straightforward conversation piece like this, which is 'low-key' dramatically, is sometimes the most appropriate form for dovetailing into a service.*

A SECRETARY *is seated at an office desk, with papers, type-writer and 'phone. Enter a stylishly dressed* BUSINESSMAN.

BUSINESSMAN: Morning, Freda.

SECRETARY: Good morning, Mr. Stevenson – here are some things for you to sign.

BUSINESSMAN: Look, I'm a bit pushed this morning, I've got this religious fellow coming to see me in a few minutes. What are they? Anything important?

SECRETARY: Well, there are those two big contracts you concluded yesterday with ICI and Lever Bros. and that cheque for five thousand pounds for the Indian Cyclone disaster.

BUSINESSMAN: Oh yes, and what about the Mercedes I saw yesterday, did you order it?

SECRETARY: Yes.

BUSINESSMAN: I must have it by the board meeting at the end of the month.

SECRETARY: In Brussels?

BUSINESSMAN: No, Paris, then Brussels. Any 'phone calls this morning?

SECRETARY: One about some investments in
Computer Services International and
one from Miss Silversmith.

BUSINESSMAN: Miss Silversmith?

SECRETARY: Your fiancée.

BUSINESSMAN: Oh yes.

SECRETARY: She was suggesting dinner with her
parents next Friday.

BUSINESSMAN: Oh dear, was she? Well, am I free?

SECRETARY: (*Flipping through diary*). No.

BUSINESSMAN: Good. I'll ring her back, then. Is that
all?

SECRETARY: Yes.

BUSINESSMAN: Righto, thanks Freda.
(*She goes, showing* JESUS *into the office
on her way out*.) Ah, hello. I'm really
pleased and honoured to have
you come to my office (*they shake
hands*) . . . I hope you won't mind me
asking you one or two questions that
have been on my mind recently. You've
got such a reputation for being a good
counsellor and I'd value some advice.

JESUS: Why do you call me good? No one is
good except God.
(*Silence. The* BUSINESSMAN *averts his
eyes from* JESUS.)

BUSINESSMAN: Hmmm. What I'm really interested in
is . . . well, you must realise that a man
in my position stands to lose a lot if I
should . . . well, er, *die* really. And so
what I'm asking is, is there any way I
can be sure that I'm not going to lose
everything . . . that I can have what you
call Eternal Life?

JESUS: You know the commandments?

BUSINESSMAN: Yes.

JESUS: Do not commit adultery . . .

BUSINESSMAN: Couldn't agree more. I'm not married
of course . . . yet, but . . .

JESUS: Do not murder, do not steal.

BUSINESSMAN: Quite, absolutely.

JESUS: Do not lie, honour your father and mother.

BUSINESSMAN: Yes, dear old things. Well, yes, I've lived my life along these sort of lines since I was a kid. I'd even go so far as to say it's been a very moral life. But all that seems rather easy, really, when one's talking about Eternal Life. A bit cheap, if you see what I mean. (*Pause*) Is that all there is to it?
(*Silence.* JESUS *looks at him.*)

JESUS: What is the most important thing in your life?

BUSINESSMAN: Well, that's hard to say, I suppose . . .

JESUS: Who has first place in your life?

BUSINESSMAN: My fiancée, I should think . . .

JESUS: Where does your security lie? In your bank balance?

BUSINESSMAN: Look, aren't we getting a bit off the subject here? I'm asking you about Eternal Life and you're just dodging the issue . . . it seems to me . . . sir.

JESUS: Is that what you really want?

BUSINESSMAN: Eternal life? Yes, I suppose so. It's not the sort of thing you can buy, though, is it? (*He gives an embarrassed laugh.*)

JESUS: You don't have to. Just come now and follow me. Obey me and share my life. (*Pause*) Are you free enough to do that?

BUSINESSMAN: Of course I'm free. I can do whatever I like.

JESUS: (*Gently*). Fine.

BUSINESSMAN: What do you mean, 'fine'?

JESUS: Well, sell all your possessions and come and follow me. (*Silence*). What's wrong?

BUSINESSMAN: You can't be serious?

JESUS: This is the only thing that stands in your way.

BUSINESSMAN: I couldn't do that.
(JESUS *leaves slowly*.)
I couldn't possibly do that . . . I couldn't do that . . . I couldn't do that . . .

The Last Judgement

THE VOICE OF CHRIST DAVE, a man relaxing at home CONNIE, a cleaner MYRTLE, a cleaner

Because of its simplicity this sketch will stand on its own and will provoke thought in virtually any situation. Choosing the best context for it, however, needs great care. Anything on the subject of judgement, particularly judgement after death, will stir up strong feelings and it may be best to perform the piece as part of a talk.

Centre stage there is a large free-standing door, facing the audience. In front of this is an armchair in which DAVE is sitting, reading the paper.

VOICE OF CHRIST: Listen. I stand at the door and knock. If anyone hears my voice and opens the door, I will come into his house and eat with him and he will eat with me. (*Knocking*)

DAVE: Can't get any peace even to read the paper these days, can yer? Who is it, anyway?

VOICE OF CHRIST: The person you've been waiting for.

DAVE: I haven't been waiting for anybody, mate.

VOICE OF CHRIST: Can I come in?

DAVE: What do you mean, 'can I come in?' This is my home. You can't just come in here. I didn't invite you. (*He continues to read the paper. Pause. The knocking begins again.*) Push off, will yer? Some people won't take no for an answer, will they? (*He gets up and goes across to the door.*) Look, mate, I don't want to seem unfriendly ... if there's anything you want ...

VOICE OF CHRIST: I want to come in.

DAVE: Well, you can't. I'm busy. Try again
when I've got more time. Try
Wednesday.
(*He sits down and reads. Silence. More
knocking.*)
This is ridiculous. How many times do
I have to tell yer? (*He gets up and goes
back to the door.*) Look, let's be
reasonable. I'm really interested in what
you've got to say. A lot of people
wouldn't even talk to you, would they?
But I'm not like that. No, I've read
your book . . . well, some of it. But
look. I'm busy and I'm tired, the wife's
busy and she's tired, the dog's busy and
he's tired – we're all tired in here, all
right? I'd love to chat for longer, but
it'll have to wait, okay?
(*He sits down again and reads. The
knocking continues, but each knock is
like ten years of his life passing. In slow
motion, following the softer and softer
beats on the door, he becomes an old
man.*)
I'm tired. (*He collapses onto the floor.*)
(*Enter* CONNIE *and* MYRTLE)

MYRTLE: You start up the stairs, Connie, and I'll
do the floor. All right, love?

CONNIE: (*Seeing the body*). 'ere Myrtle, come
and look at this.

MYRTLE: Ooh my goodness me. 'Ow long's 'e
been 'ere?

CONNIE: Day or so.

MYRTLE: Still, 'e was gettin' on.

CONNIE: Come on, let's go and get the police.
I can't stand lookin' at bodies.

MYRTLE: Makes yer think though.

CONNIE: What?

MYRTLE: Well, I always wonder where people go
when they die.
(*Exeunt. Dave slowly stirs from where he
has been lying. He looks around him,*

*bewildered. He sees the door, walks up
to it and starts to knock.*)

DAVE: Hallo? Hallo? Anyone in? It's me . . .
David. Dave. Come on, you remember
me, Davey? Hey, can I come in?
(*Silence*). We met before. At my place.
We had a chat. Remember? I talked to
you. You were going to come round
sometime. You were going to come
back . . . on Wednesday, that was it.
Remember? I said you could come
back. I said you could . . . (*He hammers
on the door.*)

VOICE OF CHRIST: Who are you?

DAVE: Dave. You remember me.

VOICE OF CHRIST: I never knew you.

(DAVE *freezes in front of the door, facing
audience.*)

The Widow's Mites: A Mime

CHRIST SOCIETY LADY RELIGIOUS MAN TYCOON WIDOW

This section is included to illustrate the section in 'Practical Guidelines': 'Sketches without Writers' (section 2). Only the roughest idea can be given but it may inspire you to explore this extremely powerful medium for yourself. The original performance of the sketch depended on accurate co-ordination with a piano backing. For this reason, one or two musical hints are given – music is not essential for mimes of this type, but 'pure mime' needs to be very good to command an audience's attention for any length of time. Costumes should be according to character but as simple as possible. CHRIST *should be dressed distinctively, in modern or symbolic costume, but not in Biblical robes unless the whole sketch is transposed for this setting. All accessories (handbags, bowls, etc.) should be mimed.*

The characters walk on and face away from the audience in a straight line. CHRIST is in the middle. The SOCIETY LADY, RELIGIOUS MAN and TYCOON stand stage right, the WIDOW stage left. Sombre music begins. At this, they all turn and face the audience. The four characters' attention is fixed on CHRIST as he steps forward. He forms a large bowl and places it on a stand. He then indicates it to the three characters on his right and steps back to watch. The music changes. A jaunty tune, anything to do with money, is appropriate (e.g. 'If I were a rich man'). The SOCIETY LADY moves confidently to the bowl, opens her handbag, takes out her purse, removes several pound notes and some loose change, and drops them in. She replaces her purse smugly, making it quite clear by her careful extraction of the money that she has not given everything. She returns to her position. CHRIST watches intently. She is followed by the RELIGIOUS MAN, who piously empties the entire contents of his wallet into the bowl, making sure that he does this in full view of the others. As he turns, he surreptitiously checks his bulging back pocket to make sure that he has plenty left over. He laughs at his ingenuity. The TYCOON now strides out. The music can change to 'Hey, big spender'. He removes his cheque book with a great flourish, selects one of his many pens, then writes a cheque with seemingly endless noughts. The others are suitably impressed, as he strides ostentatiously back to his place, looking at them patronisingly. CHRIST turns to look at the WIDOW. The music changes. It is delicate, hesitant, full of pathos. The WIDOW scarcely lifts her eyes, overcome with the inadequacy of her gift. She feels the scornful gaze of the other three bearing down on her as she searches in her bag for the two mites, one in each corner. As she drops in each mite, the piano registers it with a few, tinkling notes. She closes her bag, head bowed, and moves very slowly back to her position. The other three exchange knowing glances, but CHRIST holds up his hand in remonstrance. The sombre music returns. He steps forward, digging down into the bowl with his hands and recovering the two mites. These he takes in his left hand, and the bowl – containing the offering of the other three – in his right hand. He steps back. The music becomes more dramatic as, arms outstretched, he forms a human scales. The arms of the balance waver upwards and downwards. On the final piano chord, the WIDOW's mites bring his left arm down and his right arm up. Her total offering has outweighed all the other half-measures. The three characters are confounded. The WIDOW looks up humbly, and her gaze meets the loving expression of CHRIST.

STREET THEATRE

Street theatre is one of the most dynamic forms of communication. It has immediate dramatic impact or none at all. An obscure subject, loose timing, inadequate staging, a fluffed line, all can lose an audience. But a confident performance of a good piece of street theatre can grip the attention of a crowd longer than the most talented orator at Hyde Park Corner. People who came out to buy a packet of soap powder or to see the sights of the city will forget everything in favour of powerful (and free) entertainment. Some of the most moving relationships possible between actors and audience can be inspired by a street theatre performance, as well as a fair share of heckling and provocation. But no street theatre group, even a bad one, will have an apathetic audience. In the latter case they will have no audience at all and, if they are good, they will have an audience closely involved – moved, angered, excited or intrigued, but never indifferent.

For this reason, amongst others, street theatre is a unique opportunity to communicate clearly. It will never wash over an audience like a series of television programmes which the viewer can't be bothered to switch off, nor will it play – for that matter – to church congregations who sit glassy-eyed through a long sermon but are too polite to walk out. In street theatre, if an audience is bored, if communication has failed, then the audience moves off.

Street theatre writers and actors soon learn the hard way through experience how to retain an audience's attention, and 'experience' often means the uncomfortable feeling of a crowd looking at their watches and dispersing halfway through your programme. Audiences in the open-air, of course, are always in a state of flux, in some venues more than others, and some times of day will mean greater consistency in numbers than others, but given the best conditions it is possible to hold an audience of several hundred for half an hour or more. It is worth aiming at this in the development of a street theatre group rather than hiding behind the obvious practical difficulties. Remember: you get the attention you deserve. If a crowd walk by without a flicker of interest it is not because they have hardened their hearts to the truth but because you have either chosen the wrong venue, the wrong time, the wrong material, or the wrong actors.

Choosing a good venue. The best venues are where people are at leisure or can be encouraged to relax. City squares, public commons where people come to eat their lunch, forecourts in front of churches and pubs – anywhere, such as promenades or market-places, where people do not seem in a hurry to move elsewhere. The basic requirements are a reasonable area to perform, optimum sightlines for the audience (if a public monument with steps is available then some of the audience can be seated, if grass is chosen, then most children and some adults will sit down) and as much freedom from heavy traffic noise as possible (the hissing of air-brakes and the roar of gear-changes will make certain otherwise-suitable areas redundant for street theatre). Shopping precincts sound attractive venues to street theatre groups but vary greatly. First of all, people are there for a precise purpose and are less easily attracted and, in the second place, it is often difficult to set up a performance without obscuring at least one trader's shop window. It is wise to avoid any unnecessary antagonism of this kind. Street theatre can be anti-social if handled carelessly and should never be like a blaring transistor radio swinging from somebody's hand as they walk through a park and impose their tastes on everybody else. Try and choose somewhere where people can ignore you if they want to and where a crowd can form voluntarily, with the proviso that with any open-air activity there will often be a few unwitting members of the audience. It is against the law to use a P.A. system without official permission and, although this may be possible to obtain, to work without a P.A. helps to concentrate the crowd and reduces the chances of imposing the performance on those who are not interested. Places have such different kinds of potential that there is no 'rule of thumb' for venues except imagination and common sense: study your area and see where people gather at leisure or where there are a sufficient number of casual passers-by to attract an audience. And learn from experience. It is easy to persist in choosing a poor venue through lack of initiative.

Obtaining permission. If it is public property you will need permission from the council (written permission is best) and for this you will need to state the times and dates of your performances. It is also important that the police should be fully informed, otherwise your performance may end abruptly, albeit dramatically. If it is private property find out who it belongs to and make sure you have the owner's permission. In the case of a church forecourt, provided there is no danger of obstruction, the matter is the private concern of the church but, whilst this is so, it is a worthwhile courtesy to inform the police that you will be using the forecourt for this purpose. All these aspects of street theatre, for a Christian group, are as much part of the Christian message as the content of the programme.

Staging a performance. The first task of a street theatre performance is to gather a crowd. This can be done in a variety of ways. Colourful props, such as a painted ladder, a free-standing door or a brightly painted bill-board will create an interesting environment and in themselves may gather a crowd. Actors in costume, wearing top hats or wigs or other crazy headgear, brandishing umbrellas, riding on each others' shoulders, wearing false beards and improvising characters (preferably not more than one Long John Silver, one Richard III and one Coco the Clown to each company) can announce the forthcoming attraction to passers-by (if hand-outs are given they should be about the performance). All this will begin to gather a crowd, but most people will come when some kind of performance has started and so the first five to ten minutes are vital in creating and holding a good audience. Songs with a strong, contemporary feel towards jazz, reggae, spirituals, anything with a dynamic beat, are better than songs which would be more suitable in the context of church worship. A couple of songs with good movement (rehearsed routines if there is somebody who can choreograph them) can mean a confident relationship with the audience from the start. Following this the first sketch (or the opening scene of a street-play), should be fast moving, funny and short. The next sketch should follow without a break: in other words, a good continuity man will link from sketch to sketch briefly and to the point, welcoming everybody to the show and perhaps saying something about the group, inviting the audience to any other events that might interest them and providing that all-important thirty-second gap for two of your actors to struggle out of wild west outfits and get into Bill and Ben costumes. The ideal length for a programme is probably about twenty minutes to half-an-hour, moving from a fast, funny beginning to a serious dramatisation of the Christian message to an amusing and lively ending in a final sketch. The 'warmer' ending has some advantage in making people feel more at ease in staying to talk with the actors after the performance. A song at the end can also achieve this and may help, as other members of the company go to speak to people. Finally, once the drama has started, any songs that happen in between sketches or as part of a play must be vigorously performed as well as sung, otherwise the shift in style will mean that many people will walk off, not – in this case – because they are bored, but because they suddenly become aware of other things to do instead of being riveted by a continuous performance. The aim of the street theatre company is to make their entertainment as eye-catching and absorbing as possible.

All this, however, should never be regarded as 'cynical technique' but as a way of communicating with warmth and personal love across barriers that are normally unsurmountable, either through class, creed or prejudice.

Selecting material. Several street theatre companies use improvisation (usually bordering on slapstick) as their main stock-in-trade. In the wrong hands this can rapidly devolve into patronising nonsense which will satisfy the average crowd for a few minutes at the most, though well-handled improvisation can be impressive. It needs special care and technique. This book is concerned with written material that can be carefully rehearsed. Audiences of all ages and backgrounds, through the influence of T.V. drama, have become more sophisticated than their ancestors who revelled in the knockabout comedy. Slapstick is still as popular as ever but it should find its rightful place in street theatre as one among many kinds of entertainment. An astonishing range of dramatic effects and types of theatre, from highly stylised to naturalistic drama, from mime to morality play and panto-mime to rock musical can be explored and the sketches in this book represent only a few possibilities. In general 'wordy' sketches are less likely to work on the streets unless accompanied by very strong movement, rhythm or music. A good street theatre sketch is bold and easy to follow but not without subtlety. In addition to the sketches printed here are notes to help you write your own material (see 'Practical Guidelines').

SKETCHES FOR STREET THEATRE

The House on the Rock

NARRATOR ONE   NARRATOR TWO   FIRST WISE MAN   SECOND
WISE MAN   FIRST FOOLISH MAN   SECOND FOOLISH MAN   A FAT
PROPHET

*This style of sketch, two narrators with accompanying mime,
is very effective street theatre. As a form it has pace and
clarity, as well as a touch of music hall in the two narrators.
The following are only suggestions for costumes: miner's hat
for* FIRST WISE MAN, *topee and moustache for* SECOND WISE
MAN, *silly mask or animal costume for* FIRST FOOLISH MAN,
clown suit and red nose for SECOND FOOLISH MAN, *long beard
and Biblical robes for* FAT PROPHET. *The* SECOND WISE MAN
*could easily be played as an ordinary workman. Imagination
should be used in deciding all this and working out the individual movements of the mime. It goes without saying that
most street theatre sketches like this can be performed indoors.*

*A free-standing door upstage centre is a good idea for exits
and entrances. Enter* NARRATORS:

ONE: Jesus said
TWO: Anyone who hears my words
ONE: And does something about them
TWO: Is like a wise man
ONE: Who built
TWO: His house
ONE: Upon
TWO: A rock
ONE: A rock.
TWO: Rockety-rock-rock
ONE: Rock-rock.
TWO: Who's there?
   (*Enter* FIRST WISE MAN)
ONE: A wise man building his house upon a
   rock.

TWO: Rock on, baby.

ONE: He built slowly and carefully

TWO: Steadily and firmly

ONE: First, the foundations.

TWO: Then ... more foundations.

ONE: Then ... more foundations.

TWO: And finally he built himself

ONE: A cave.

TWO: So we sacked him (FIRST WISE MAN *is ushered off, reluctantly*).

ONE: And got ourselves a new wise man (*Enter* SECOND WISE MAN)

TWO: Who built slowly and carefully

ONE: Steadily and firmly.

TWO: Meanwhile, back on the beach

ONE: There was a foolish man (*Enter* FIRST FOOLISH MAN)

TWO: (*Silly voice*) Hulloo!

ONE: He was like a person ...

TWO: But he wasn't in fact.

ONE: So we sacked him (FIRST FOOLISH MAN *is ushered off*).

TWO: And got ourselves a new foolish man. (*Enter* SECOND FOOLISH MAN)

ONE: He was like a person who hears what Jesus says

TWO: And does nothing about it.

ONE: But he had plenty of ideas about building.

TWO: A lot of know-how.

ONE: Plenty of experience.

TWO: Many kinds of experience.

ONE: He was open-minded.

TWO: Broad-minded.

ONE: Clear-sighted.

TWO: Hard-headed.

ONE: But not hard up.

TWO: He had a finger in every pie

ONE: And a head in every pudding.

TWO: And so he built his house upon the sand.

ONE: Because it was nearest.

TWO: And planned to rent it out

ONE: To a fat profit.
    (*Enter* FAT PROPHET. *Both* NARRATORS *are puzzled.*)

TWO: (*Perusing his script, if one is used, or otherwise realising the mistake*). Er . . . sorry, planned to rent it out *at* a fat profit.
    (*Exit disappointed* FAT PROPHET)

ONE: So, there they were.

TWO: The wise man

ONE: And the foolish man

TWO: Building their houses

ONE: One on the rock

TWO: And the other on the sand.

ONE: And then

TWO: It started

ONE: Raining.
    (*The two* NARRATORS *give umbrellas to the* WISE MAN *and the* FOOLISH MAN. *The latter's umbrella is in a state of disrepair. He further compounds his folly by holding it upside down.*)

TWO: And the rain came down.

ONE: And the floods came up.

TWO: And the rain came down.

ONE: And the floods came up.

TWO: And the rain came up.

ONE: And fooled everybody.

TWO: Including the foolish man

ONE: Who was pretty fooled anyway.

TWO: And so it went on

ONE: And on

TWO: And on

ONE: And on

TWO: And on

ONE: Raining.

TWO: (*Sound of gurgling water*).

ONE: (*More gurgling water*).

TWO: And a strong wind blew up. BANG!

ONE: So we had to get another one.

TWO: And it blew

ONE: And it blew

TWO: And it yellow

ONE: And it blew.

TWO: And the house on the sand fell . . .
(*The* FOOLISH MAN *falls.*)

ONE: Flat! Crash bang!

TWO: Pity.

ONE: Oh dear.

TWO: Tinkle smash.

ONE: Because it had no foundation.

TWO: And the foolish man drowned. (*Sound of water going down a plug-hole.*)

ONE: But the wise man

TWO: Stepped out of his house

ONE: Which hadn't budged an inch

TWO: And made himself

ONE: A cup of tea

TWO: With two sugars

ONE: On *the rock.*

The Story of King Josiah

NARRATOR JOSIAH, the young king of Judah HILKIAH, the High Priest SHAPHAN, the secretary, somewhat officious but eager to please MR. O'CONNOR, supervisor of Temple Renovation LAD, his half-witted assistant CHORUS, anything from five to fifteen people

This sketch was originally written for a Scripture Union cassette intended for children, but it has worked very well as a street theatre piece. The main device for its performance has been the use of a group mime (see a further development of this technique in THE PARABLE OF THE GOOD PUNK ROCKER) acting like a constant echo of the script. Certain uses of the group mime will be included in the stage directions, but imagination is needed to develop the actions along the lines suggested.

The CHORUS should be dressed identically (we have usually worn black trousers and pullover with a Star of David emblem as a breast-piece). JOSIAH, HILKIAH and SHAPHAN can justifiably wear Biblical costumes in this piece, but for those afraid of incongruity (rarely a problem in street theatre) something should be designed. MR. O'CONNOR and THE LAD should be dressed in building site overalls and helmets. The CHORUS makes a circle, facing inwards, around JOSIAH.

> NARRATOR: The story of King Josiah!
> (*The circle breaks open and* JOSIAH *steps forward.*)
> There was once a king whose name means God-looks-after-me.
> CHORUS: (*Repeating, with appropriate actions*).
> God-looks-after-me.
> NARRATOR: He was called Josiah in Hebrew and he was King of Judah. (*The* CHORUS *bow to him.*) Though he was young he called the entire nation back to God and obedience to his word (CHORUS *actions*).

Silence for the King! (*A trumpet blast if available*).

JOSIAH: People of Judah! Do you realise that not everybody in this country is worshipping God? Instead, they prefer to worship bits of stone and bronze.

CHORUS: (*Scandalised*). Stone and bronze?! Stone and bronze?!

JOSIAH: You know what I think about this. (*They nod vigorously.*) It makes my blood boil!! (*Sound of blood boiling, top blowing, etc.*). This nation belongs to God and it's about time we paid him more respect. From today we shall renovate the temple. Hilkiah, priest of the Most High God (*enter* HILKIAH), you will be in charge of the operation and you, Shaphan (*enter* SHAPHAN) my right hand man (*but* SHAPHAN *has gone to the left hand side, where* HILKIAH *is already standing*) – my *right* hand man (SHAPHAN *moves apologetically to the right*), will keep me in touch with all the plan.

(HILKIAH *mutters something to* SHAPHAN, *who hurries off obsequiously. He moves off in the other direction. Enter* MR. O'CONNOR *and* LAD. *In this scene of renovating the temple, they use the members of the* CHORUS *like blocks of stone, moving them into position.*)

MR. O'CONNOR: Renovate the temple – right, sir. Now over here, lad, we've got to fix back in all those jewels, repair the south wall and get that gold shining on the lintels, and it's a very tricky job because this wall might collapse at any moment. (*The* LAD *pushes all the pieces into position, but the* CHORUS *sway around, creaking and groaning, and eventually collapse.*) Shiver me timbers!

LAD: I just have, sir.

MR. O'CONNOR: Yes, you prize idiot, I can see that.
(*As this exchange is going on, the*
CHORUS *are acting like a machine – a*
clockwork mechanism, producing a box
from a secret panel – set off by the
disaster.)

LAD: Hey, excuse me sir, Mr. O'Connor . . .
Mr. O'Connor? There's a secret panel
in here and there's a box in it.

MR. O'CONNOR: So there is, lad.

LAD: Shall I take it to the High Priest?

MR. O'CONNOR: Yes, and remember to say 'Your Grace'.

LAD: 'For what we are about to receive, may
the—'

MR. O'CONNOR: No, not that, 'Your Grace', 'Your
Highness'.

LAD: Oh yes.
(MR. O'CONNOR *goes off, shaking his head*
despairingly. The LAD *runs off to*
HILKIAH. *He should run round the*
CHORUS, *who get up off the ground,*
resuming their line. They all run on the
spot breathlessly, echoing his movements.
Enter HILKIAH, *meeting the* LAD *in front*
of the CHORUS.)

LAD: Excuse me, for what we're ab – I mean,
Your Grace, we found this box in a
secret panel! Maybe there's a fortune
inside! Rubies!

CHORUS: Cor!

LAD: Pearls!

CHORUS: Wow!

LAD: Gold!!

CHORUS: Zap!!
(HILKIAH *removes an old scroll, blowing*
off the dust. They all cough.)

LAD: Eugh! It's just an old scroll. (*He goes*).

HILKIAH: This has been left in here for many
years – let's have a read: 'Hear, O
people, what the Lord says, the Lord
our God is one Lord, and you shall

love the Lord your God with all your heart.' THIS IS THE BOOK OF THE LAW! Call the King's secretary.

CHORUS: (*Four voices in succession*). Call the King's secretary!

SHAPHAN: (*Running on efficiently*). Call the King's secretary! – Oh, wait a minute, that's me. I am the King's secretary. (*Bowing to* HILKIAH). Your Grace?

HILKIAH: I've found the Book of the Law. These are the words of God to all people and they've been hidden in a little box and nobody's been able to find them for years!
(*During the following sequence of exchanges, the* CHORUS *follow the remarks like a ball at a tennis match:*)

SHAPHAN: The Book of the Law!

HILKIAH: It's incredible!

SHAPHAN: It's amazing!

HILKIAH: THE BOOK OF THE LAW!

SHAPHAN: Exactly.

HILKIAH: It's quite amazing.

SHAPHAN: Shall I ring the bells?

HILKIAH: You don't understand. This is a *terrible* disaster.

CHORUS: (*Recoiling in alarm*). Aaaaaaaargh!!

SHAPHAN: What? A disaster?

HILKIAH: A TERRIBLE disaster.

CHORUS: (*Recoiling even further*). AAAAAAAAARGH!!

HILKIAH: We've found the Book of the Law hidden in a box.

SHAPHAN: Precisely.

HILKIAH: Which means that nobody's been reading the Book of the Law.

SHAPHAN: Oh yes, I hadn't thought of that.

HILKIAH: Which means that God will be very angry and disappointed. There's no time to lose – take this to the King immediately.

SHAPHAN: I shall take it in person, Your Grace.

Oh dear, what a palaver (*he runs round
the* CHORUS *twice during this, and they
form a background to his anxiety by
furrowing their brows, beating their
breasts, biting their nails, etc., and
chanting: 'oh dear, oh dear . . .'*) Oh dear,
oh dear, King Josiah is going to be
very upset by this, I know it, I know it.
He could fly completely off the handle.
Oh dear, to think that God went to all
the trouble of having this book written
and nobody's been reading it. Oh dear,
oh dear. (*He arrives in front of the*
CHORUS. JOSIAH *has entered. He presses
an imaginary door-bell.*)

CHORUS: Bing-bong.

JOSIAH: Come in.

SHAPHAN: (*Entering and prostrating himself*). Oh
King live for ever, may your name be
honoured among all men, your royal
sceptre holding sway throughout the
earth, your unrivalled magnificence be—

JOSIAH: (*Wearily*). Yes, yes, quite so, Shaphan.
Now what is it?

SHAPHAN: (*Getting up immediately*). Your Majesty,
a terrible disaster!

CHORUS: AAAARGH!

JOSIAH: What's that?

SHAPHAN: It's this you see. We've found it.

JOSIAH: Found what?

SHAPHAN: The disaster – I mean, listen to this.
(*Unravelling the scroll*). I quote: 'The
Lord our God is one Lord and you
shall love the Lord with all your heart
and all your soul and with all your
might. And these are the—'

JOSIAH: It's the Book of the Law! You've found
it! This is wonderful!
(*The* CHORUS *do a victorious dance
routine, with a chant, ending in some
flamboyant pose* (*see big band intro-
ductions to famous stars in T.V. shows.*))

SHAPHAN: Well, it was . . . er . . . nothing really,

I'm glad to be of service.

JOSIAH: But Shaphan! Don't you realise? It's terrible!

CHORUS: (*Recoiling*). Aaaaaargh!

SHAPHAN: (*Utterly perplexed*). Terrible??!

JOSIAH: Wonderful *and* terrible.
(*The* CHORUS *do a combination of the 'wonderful' and 'terrible' effects, a kind of 'hey-hey!-Aaaargh!'.*)

JOSIAH: Wonderful because now we can read God's word and obey it, terrible because it shows us all the things we've forgotten about! Oh God forgive us.
(JOSIAH *falls to his knees, followed by the* CHORUS.)

SHAPHAN: (*To the audience, still standing*). I knew he'd get upset – I told you.
(JOSIAH *pulls him to his knees, and he immediately starts praying with exaggerated piety.*)

JOSIAH: Forgive us for not reading your word and not listening to what you have to say. Oh how can he ever forgive us? Dear God, you've helped me in everything and now I can see that we have failed you. Help me to put everything right.

NARRATOR: Immediately Josiah set to work. He had a public reading of the Book of the Law, when everybody in his country came and listened to God's word. All the people agreed to follow the King's example, to read God's word and to obey it.

CHORUS: (*Voices in succession*). The Law of the Lord is perfect, reviving the soul! The Testimony of the Lord is sure, making wise the simple! The precepts of the Lord are right, rejoicing the heart! The Commandment of the Lord is pure, enlightening the eyes!
(*The last sequence in our performances*

*of 'JOSIAH' has been a song,
accompanied by a group mime. The mime
has been, effectively, a 'machine' – a
series of inter-acting movements from
each player, all based on building the
temple: brick-laying, hammering,
painting, sawing, cement mixing, etc.
To sing and move vigorously at the same
time requires practice, especially to
achieve clarity and volume. Guitar
backing is a good idea in the streets. The
following are the words of a chorus,
known to many church groups, but
adapted for the theme of the sketch:*)

The Law of the Lord
Is written in the Bible,
The way that He shows
His love to all the people.
If you want to find out
What God is like
You must read God's book,
To see the light and know what's right,
You must read God's book.
The Law of the Lord
Is written in the Bible,
The way that He shows
His love to all the people
If you think you've read it all before
Then read it again,
If you've never even read it at all,
IT'S TIME YOU BEGAN.

(*The last line is shouted out, and the*
CHORUS *break up the 'machine' to point
out to the audience on the final syllable.
All the cast, as well as the* CHORUS,
*should be involved in the 'public reading'
and the song.*)

Violence in the Home

T.V. ANNOUNCER   MOTHER   FATHER   DAUGHTER   SON

*The teaching of Jesus was often aimed at the 'law-abiding'
citizen who felt self-righteous. The sketch typifies this familiar
attitude of detachment from the evil in the world, a habit of
mind frequently worsened by television viewing. In addition to
its relevance, an actor sitting behind a hollowed out television
set and reading the news is a useful eye-catcher for street
audiences. For another use of the television set, see ONE FOR
ME AND NONE FOR YOU p. 30.*

*The stage setting is an ordinary living room. For open air
performance, no more is needed than a few surfaces to sit on,
chairs if available, and the television set with the* ANNOUNCER
seated behind it. The SON *lounges across two chairs, the*
DAUGHTER *sits disconsolately, the* MOTHER *goes over to switch
on the news.*

ANNOUNCER: Good evening. Tragedy hits a home in
North London. A man was arrested
today after attacking his wife and two
children with a sledge hammer. All
three have since died. The children,
Richard aged nine, and Elizabeth aged
eight, had recently been sent to a new
school but had come home for the
holidays. The man, John Harris,
thirty-one, said earlier today, 'I didn't
mean to kill them. I got annoyed. I lost
control.' He pleaded not guilty to
charges of violence with intent to kill.
More news about the threatened strike
at British Leyland. . . .
(MOTHER *switches off television.*)
MOTHER: I think it's terrible that anybody should
do that. There's nothing but violence on
the news. How could anybody do that?

I don't see how a man could just go and kill his wife and children.

(*Enter* HUSBAND)

Why are you late? You said you'd be here at four o'clock. You never come when you say. I wanted us to go shopping together this afternoon. You never think of others, do you? – You're so selfish!

(*As she says this, she points at him to emphasise her words. The* HUSBAND *dies as if he were shot by a gun.*)

(*In some circumstances, the damaging nature of swear-words can be indicated by adding one to 'selfish' – we have generally done this on the streets and in clubs, but not in church, where attitudes of anger rather than specific bad language tend to be the problem. It can be right to demonstrate the implications of swearing in anger, but it is senseless to cause offence by doing this if the problem is not a relevant one.*)

VOICE: (*During this the action freezes*). You want things but you cannot have them so you quarrel and fight. You want things and you cannot get them so you are ready to kill.

MOTHER: (*As her daughter gets up to go*). You're not going out looking like that, are you? That dress hangs on you like a sack. Why can't you be like Claire next door? She's got real taste.

(*The* DAUGHTER *dies. Freeze.*)

VOICE: The tongue is like a fire. It is a world of wrong spreading evil through our whole being. No man has ever been able to control it.

(*The* MOTHER, *oblivious to the effect of her words, turns to her son:*)

MOTHER: Out! Go on, get out! After all I've done for you, you sit on your backside lazing

around. You make me sick!
(*The* SON *falls off the chair and dies.
Freeze.*)

VOICE: You have been told 'do not murder'.
But I say to you, anyone who is angry
with his brother has already committed
murder.
(*The* MOTHER *goes over and switches on
the television.*)

ANNOUNCER: Good evening. Here is the late news.
Tragedy hits a home in North London.
A man was arrested today after attacking
his wife and two children with a sledge
hammer. All three have since died. The
children, Richard aged nine, and
Elizabeth aged eight, had recently
been sent to a new school but had come
home for the holidays. The man, John
Harris, thirty-one, said earlier today,
'I didn't mean to kill them. I got
annoyed. I lost control.' He pleaded not
guilty to charges of violence with intent
to kill. (*The* MOTHER *switches off the
television.*)

MOTHER: (*To the audience*). How can anybody do
a thing like that?

The Light of the World

PEOPLE, four men and two women   CHRIST   NARRATOR

Although the barest outline of all the sketches published in this book, this piece has probably had the greatest impact. It has derived this from vivid stylisation alongside the simple truths of the gospel. The stage directions can only convey a rough idea of the sketch in performance; it is really presented for your own interpretation and as an example of the use of scripture in dramatic performance.

The PEOPLE *should be dressed in black. Their number and sexes could differ from the recommendation here (for example, two men and four girls), but the maximum number of people would be nine, making up three groups.* CHRIST *should be dressed in modern costume, either in black or in another simple outfit: red trousers and white shirt are often the most effective. The action of the mime takes place round a ladder. The opening 'frame' is the figure of* CHRIST, *standing towards the top of the ladder, but facing away from the audience, whilst the six actors hunch down as low as they can, facing towards the audience (but their faces hidden in their hands). For the first half of the sketch they are in two groups, with one girl to each group – and both these groups are now formed stage left and stage right.*

NARRATOR: No one has seen God.
(The two groups come to life, but their hands still shield their eyes, blindfolding them from God.)
But God became a human being and lived among us.
(CHRIST *turns and faces the audience.*)
He was full of truth and light.
(As he descends the ladder:)
The light has come into the world, but men loved the darkness rather than the light because they do evil things.

(*The* PEOPLE *are stung by the presence of
the light and retreat into their groups,
occupying themselves with evil.*)

And anyone who does evil things hates
the pure light and will not come to the
light, because he doesn't want his evil
deeds to be shown up.

(*Lovingly,* CHRIST *attempts to make
contact but he is repelled by the* PEOPLE,
*who freeze into positions of perverse
delight in evil and protection of their
lives from the influence of* CHRIST. *In the
stillness,* CHRIST *stretches out his hands,
as if to shine in the world despite the
unresponsiveness of human hearts. As he
does this, the* NARRATOR *says:*)

The light shines in the darkness of the
evil of men's hearts – where the trouble
begins.

(*A drum begins to beat, simulating the
human heart. As the* NARRATOR *says the
next line, the* PEOPLE *relax into neutral
positions:*)

Out of the heart of every man comes:

(*The catalogue of sins are presented like
a series of ten snapshots; they should be
carefully worked on for the maximum
uniqueness of each pose. Freeze each
time long enough for the audience to take
the image into account. Throughout this,
the 'heart' continues beating.*)

Evil thoughts
Lust
Murder
Adultery
Deceit
Envy
Scandalmongering
Pride
Foolishness
Violence

(*During this sequence,* CHRIST *has faced*

*away and is lashed by each sin as if he
were being flogged before the crucifixion.
As the* NARRATOR *says the following
line, the groups relax the last pose and
stand in a crescent from stage right to
stage left, with the central actors slightly
nearer the audience:*)

This is why the heart of man must be
changed –

Not the world

(*The actors point out to the world around
them, as a single movement starting with
the actor standing farthest stage left, and
moving through the group like a wave.*)

Not history

(*Any suitable positions e.g. reading
books, backward glances.*)

Not governments

(*Each actor stamps his foot and raises
his right hand in salute.*)

Not the economic situation

(*Everyone is penniless.*)

Not the newspaper headlines

(*Some read newspapers, others mime
newsvending.*)

Not the man next door

(*Everyone points to someone else.*)

Not your wife

(*The men point to the women.*)

Your husband

(*The women point to the men.*)

But you – you – you – you – you.

(*On each 'you' the actors point to
different people, first to one another,
then to themselves, then to different
parts of the audience, and on the final
'you' they all shout it with the* NARRATOR
as they swing round and point to CHRIST.
*Stamping their feet, and hammering
their fists into the air, they close in on*
CHRIST *and beat him back up the ladder.
They crucify him, the accelerating drum*

*beats suddenly becoming the hammer
blows of nails into his hands. Exhausted,
they all drop down to the foot of the
ladder, heads bowed as* CHRIST *hangs on
the cross. His head drops forward
as he dies. There is*
silence. *Music, if available, can be
played softly – perhaps the best is a
human voice singing a lament very
quietly, but there should be nothing
forced or sentimental. Gradually, two of
the men raise their heads, then stand to
take* CHRIST *down from the cross. They
lower him into a circle of standing
figures, facing inwards, where he is
hidden from the audience. Once this new
group has been formed, the* NARRATOR
speaks:)

Your life must be changed. You must
start all over again. And this is possible
because Jesus, who was perfect, died in
our place. He paid the penalty for the
evil in our hearts so that we might live.
He gave the light for the darkness.
(*At this, the circle of figures breaks open
and* CHRIST *steps forward.*)
The light shines in the darkness and the
darkness has never put it out.
(*Now all the* PEOPLE *are gathered round*
CHRIST. *Some stand, others sit. All look
at him, as he turns to look out at the
audience. The final 'frame' should not
be a stilted arrangement of people, like a
team photograph, but the relaxed and
welcoming impression of a family.*)

The Unforgiving Servant

NARRATOR ONE   NARRATOR TWO   OFFICE CLERK   KING   SERVANT
FRIEND   TWO ARMED GUARDS

*See the introduction to THE HOUSE ON THE ROCK.
This sketch has a similar cartoon element, which should be
highlighted in the extreme contrast between the two debts.
The* SERVANT *should have a large sackful hung round his neck,
inscribed 'massive great big debt' and his* FRIEND *should have
a tiny little bag round his neck labelled '£5'. It is worth
pointing out that, despite similarities, this sketch, and particularly THE PARABLE OF THE TALENTS, have been
more accessible to children than THE HOUSE ON THE
ROCK, which is possibly a little more 'off-beat' in its humour.
The two* NARRATORS *should be dressed identically – boaters
and blazers, top hat and tails, evening dress, etc.*

*The use of the free-standing door is helpful. There is also a
table centre-stage, covered with official looking documents.
Enter* OFFICE CLERK, *a nervous looking bureaucrat, who
approaches his desk punctiliously. He sits down. Arranges his
papers, removes the top from his pen and looks at* NARRATOR
TWO. *This gets him off to a bad start, because* NARRATOR ONE
*is the first to speak, and the little sequence that follows finally
leaves him in a state of emotional and mental panic.*

> ONE: Problem.
> *(The* OFFICE CLERK *swivels round to face*
> NARRATOR ONE.)
> TWO: How often must I forgive someone who
> hurts me?
> *(He swivels round to face* NARRATOR
> TWO.)
> ONE: Think of a number.
> *(Already confused, the* OFFICE CLERK
> *racks his brains, shuffling through his
> papers.)*
> TWO: Umm . . . Oooh . . . errr . . . errr . . . Six.

(*The* OFFICE CLERK *produces the number on a large sheet of paper.*)

ONE: Think of a bigger number.

TWO: Errr ... oooh ... oooh dear ... errr ... Seven.

(*The* OFFICE CLERK *triumphantly produces a number seven.*)

ONE: Multiply it by seventy.

TWO: Divide it by the square root of your 'phone number.

ONE: Double it.

TWO: Treble it.

ONE: Scribble it.

TWO: Add two.

ONE: Take away three.

TWO: Add one.

ONE: And what have you got?

(*The* OFFICE CLERK *is slumped across his desk, enmeshed in a spaghetti of administrative confusion. He timidly raises a hand.*)

TWO: Errr ... Can we go fru dat agen, please?

ONE: Okay, okay, start again, start again.

TWO: Putting it another way ...

(*The* OFFICE CLERK *retires gratefully, taking his desk and papers with him.*)

ONE: The disciple Peter said to Jesus:

TWO: How often must I forgive someone who hurts me?

ONE: And Jesus said to Peter:

TWO: Think of a number too big to think of.

ONE: And while Peter was thinking,

TWO: Jesus told the following story:

ONE: The Kingdom of Heaven

TWO: Is rather like

ONE: This.

TWO: There was a king.

(*Enter* KING *computing accounts with a notebook and pencil.*)

Settling accounts with his servants.

ONE: And there was a servant

TWO: Settling accounts with the king.

(*Enter* SERVANT *with enormous debt hung round his neck.*)

ONE: And the servant owed the king some money.

TWO: Quite a lot of money, really.

ONE: Loads and loads of it, in fact.

TWO: Hundreds!

ONE: Thousands!

TWO: Millions!

ONE: Well anyway, it was a lot of money.

TWO: For a chap like him.

ONE: A massive great big debt.

TWO: Hanging round his neck.

ONE: And he knew that he couldn't pay

TWO: And the king knew that he couldn't pay

ONE: And he knew that the king knew that he knew he couldn't pay.

TWO: Which was pretty bad news.

ONE: So the king ordered him to be sold as a slave.

TWO: And his wife

ONE: And his children

TWO: And all that he possessed.

ONE: To go to the liquidators.

TWO: 'Five quid for his shirt!'

ONE: 'Six quid for his shoes!'

TWO: 'Twenty five "p" for his socks!'

ONE: (*Holding his nose*). No, leave the socks, mate.

TWO: 'Stop!' He shouted.

ONE: And he fell on his knees – clunk!

TWO: And implored the king to have patience with him.

ONE: 'Have patience with me!'

TWO: He implored.

ONE: 'And I will pay you everything!'

TWO: A likely story.

ONE: But seeing the poor man's distress

TWO: The king was deeply moved.

(*The* KING *removes a handkerchief, wipes tears from his eyes, wrings out the handkerchief and replaces it.*)

ONE: In one short moment he forgave the
man the whole debt!

TWO: The whole lot.
(*The* KING *strikes out the debt and leaves.*)

ONE: Forgiven.

TWO: In a moment.

ONE: Just like that.

TWO: Wow!

ONE: Cor!

TWO: Incredible!

ONE: Too much!

TWO: Needless to say, the man was very
pleased

ONE: And he went on his way, merrily
(NARRATOR ONE *whistles nonchalantly*).

TWO: On his way, he bumped into a friend.
(*Enter* FRIEND)

ONE: Who owed him a fiver.

TWO: 'Aha! You owe me five quid,' he cried.

ONE: Seizing him briskly by the throat.

TWO: What do you say to that?

ONE: (*Strangled noise*).

TWO: That's no excuse!

ONE: But the man fell on his knees – clunk!

TWO: And implored the servant to have
patience with him.

ONE: 'Have patience with me!'

TWO: He implored.

ONE: 'And I will pay you everything!'

TWO: But, ignoring the poor man's distress,

ONE: He flung him into jail

TWO: Until the debt was paid in full.
(*The* SERVANT *drags his* FRIEND *by the
scruff of the neck and throws him off
stage.*)

ONE: But the king

TWO: Who kept his ears to the ground
(*Enter* KING, *listening to the ground.*)

ONE: Heard about this

TWO: And what he heard made him extremely
angry.

ONE: In anger he summoned the servant before him.

TWO: 'You wicked servant!'

ONE: He said, angrily.

TWO: 'Think of all that I forgave you.

ONE: Think of what you refused to forgive.

TWO: I showed you mercy.

ONE: You showed him none.

TWO: Therefore I will show you none.'

ONE: And the servant was sent to jail.
(*Enter* TWO ARMED GUARDS *who remove the trembling* SERVANT.)

TWO: Where he would be very well looked after.

ONE: (*He laughs knowingly*). Nya, nya, nya, nya . . .

TWO: Until his debt was paid in full.

ONE: And the king said:
(*The* KING *comes forward, as if to address the audience*.)

TWO: 'Think carefully.

ONE: This will happen to you as well,

TWO: If you do not forgive your brother

ONE: From your heart.'

The Parable of the Good Punk Rocker

NARRATOR CHORUS, anything from five to fifteen actors

This is a difficult sketch to transcribe, probably because it is the very opposite of a 'literary' style. It is a theatrical piece which depends on very strong chorus inter-action, arranged round the rhythm of a railway train. Rhythm is present in all theatre in some form or another, usually through speech rhythms, but here it is deliberately exaggerated as a means of communicating memorably – just as the strong rhythms of nursery rhymes with chorus actions are so easy to remember. The piece is an attempt to put the story of the Good Samaritan into the context of an alienated member of modern society, but naturally – as fashions change – the sketch could be adapted. Despite the limitations of a printed version, this style can be highly recommended for street theatre.

The piece is performed by the chorus from which the principal parts emerge when required. The NARRATOR *should be one of the chorus and act as its leader. 'RHYTHM' indicates the sound of a railway train made by the chorus with their hands slapping their thighs, 'FX' is shorthand for appropriate sound effects and actions. Each group will need to work out for itself the precise cues for the rhythm starting and finishing.*

NARRATOR: A man was on a train from London to York. (*RHYTHM*)

CHORUS: London to York – London to York – London to York – London to York.

NARRATOR: And as he sat down to read the newspaper he fell among football fans.

CHORUS: (*FX. Football chant (clapping rather than singing). Repeat.*)

NARRATOR: Who had just seen their team lose the cup.

CHORUS: BOO!! What a load of rubbish! (*Sung rather than said*).

NARRATOR: So they mugged the man and took his wallet and his coat.
(*Four of the* CHORUS *mug the man with stylised blows accompanied by:*)

CHORUS: OOH-OOH, AAH-AAH, OOH-OOH, AAH-AAH. (*FX. Football chant:*)
You'll never walk again, a-gain. (*RHYTHM*)

NARRATOR: Now on that train there was a vicar.

CHORUS: (*Singing*) A – a – men.

NARRATOR: Who felt sorry for the man.

CHORUS: (*FX. Four sniffs*)

NARRATOR: So he hid in the lavatory and said a prayer.

CHORUS: SLAM! CLICK! (*The sounds are produced, rather than the words being said but there should be accompanying actions.*)
(*RHYTHM*)

NARRATOR: And also on that train there was a social worker from Camden Town who had wide experience with delinquents.

VOICE: I really care about the kids (*She takes a drag on her fag*).

CHORUS: I really care about the kids (*They all take a drag*).

NARRATOR: She cared so much about the kids that she went to the bar and had a drink.

CHORUS: (*FX. Gulp*)
(*RHYTHM.*)

NARRATOR: Also on the train there was the leader of a punk rock group called 'The Dregs'.

CHORUS: (*FX. Punk Rock*)

NARRATOR: He was the meanest of the mean no-good guys.

CHORUS: (*FX. Throwing up* (*or something else suitably off-putting*).)

NARRATOR: But he stopped the train.

CHORUS: (*FX. Screech. Hiss.*)

NARRATOR: 'Phoned the ambulance.

CHORUS: (*FX. 'Phoning, followed by approaching siren.*)

NARRATOR: Gave him twenty quid for a new coat.

CHORUS: (*Sympathetically*). Ahhh!

NARRATOR: And sent him off to hospital.

CHORUS: (*FX. Siren fading off.*)

NARRATOR: Now where that man came from there were no punk rockers.

CHORUS: (*FX. Scandalised uppercrust:*) 'eaohh!'

NARRATOR: But there was a vicar.

CHORUS: (*Singing*) A – a – men.

NARRATOR: And several social workers.

CHORUS: I really care about the kids (*They all take a drag*).

NARRATOR: But when it came to the crunch.

CHORUS: (*FX. Loud crunch*)

NARRATOR: Who was that man's real next door neighbour?

VOICE: Sir . . . sir . . . please, sir!

NARRATOR: Yes, Nigel.

VOICE: The one that *did* something for him!

CHORUS: Oh yes! The one that *did* something for him!

NARRATOR: Who showed love, love, love, love, love, love, love.

CHORUS: Love, love, love, love, love, love, love.

NARRATOR: Jesus said:

CHORUS: (*All pointing out to the audience*). Go!!

NARRATOR: And do the same.

CHORUS: Love, love, love, love, love, your neighbour! (*Hugging each other*). Love, love, love, love, love your neighbour!

VOICE: (*Plaintively*). Sir . . . sir . . . please, sir?

NARRATOR: (*Patiently*). What is it, Nigel?

VOICE: Who is my neighbour, sir?

NARRATOR: Two, three:

CHORUS: EVERYBODY!!

VOICE: Oh yeah (*he laughs idiotically*) . . . (*RHYTHM. GRADUALLY FADING OFF.*)

THE BIBLE AND DRAMA

God's Word is Active

The Bible is often referred to as 'the Word of God', but John's Gospel speaks of Jesus Christ as the Word 'which became flesh and dwelt among us'. This is a statement for all time that God's Word is not a question of theory, a mere utterance, but is living and active, 'sharper than a two-edged sword'. The Bible is not so much a book of words but a book of actions, the actions of a Creator-God who is dramatic, who causes, who enters, who alters, who decides and who exemplifies his purposes clearly to human beings. God's ultimate action was the incarnation of the Messiah in human form.

The Bible therefore affirms that 'word' and 'action' are inextricably linked. Even the Hebrew word 'dabar' means both 'word' and 'action'. The Bible is a poor manual for anyone interested in abstract philosophical speculation but it is a constant inspiration to all who wish to live out the life of the Spirit and, furthermore, it is inspiration to those who seek to communicate God's Word with clarity today.

There are numerous instances in the Bible of words being used in a way which goes beyond that of mere information. In fact, there are only very few passages – perhaps some genealogies and tabulations of laws – where words are simply 'functional'. It's as if God's messages to man naturally find a form which is often an image, an illustration, a picture, a poem, a story told simply and dramatically. And it is no coincidence that Jesus, who was both the medium and the message of salvation, helped people to receive his words by telling them unforgettable parables and stories.

Christians have often emphasised *what* is said rather than *how* it is said, with fatal consequences. Life is not all 'head', it is body, mind, spirit and soul. We need to convey the Christian message in such a way that it will speak to the whole man. A careful study of the Bible is the best possible education for anybody wishing to do this.

The Techniques of the Prophets

The prophets knew how to use words memorably so that the record of the Divine Will would stand the test of time, despite its frequent initial rejection. Their prophecies were couched in poetic form and contained every conceivable literary device: puns, assonance, imagery, symbolism, quotations, irony, sarcasm, and some of the greatest lyrical genius. Not only did they speak the word of God but they spoke it with artistry – with God-inspired technique. They knew their contemporary culture and they knew how to speak words which would plunge like shafts of steel into the hardest of hearts or would reach with loving sympathy into the most desolate of predicaments. And as well as speaking powerfully, they often added strength to their message by performing symbolic actions: Ahijah's sign to Jeroboam of the coat rent in pieces, Elijah's sign to Joash with the bow and arrows, Isaiah's naming of his sons, Hosea's marriage to Gomer, Jeremiah's breaking of the potter's vessel, Ezekiel's brick-siege of Jerusalem. Nobody that God intended to hear his Word could have failed to understand their message, though many refused to obey it.

The Psalms in Performance

Certain psalms suggest far more colour and ritual in their original context than we would dare to give them in our church services. We have often reduced them to the palest echo of the shouts of rejoicing, the confident processions, or the dramatic cries to God which may have been part of their performance in ancient Israel. Psalm 24 is a good example of a liturgy containing elements of dramatic form and some of the oldest psalm literature, such as the Song of Deborah, are intriguing in this respect.

This subject is a question of historical debate and opinions vary greatly as to the degree of 'dramatic' involvement there may have been in such ancient texts, but the Bible itself clearly indicates that some of these pieces were written to include music, dance and procession. Even if none of this was the case the very words of the psalms and other books like Job or the Song of Solomon demonstrate a powerful dramatic imagination: a literary form that sees conflicts, that asks questions and poses answers, that characterises 'the arrogant' or delights the heart of the lover with descriptions of her beloved.

The New Testament

In a book of sketches, so many of which are based on material from the gospels, it is superfluous to point out the dramatic nature of the gospel narratives. Yet this is sometimes overlooked by Christians who regard the theoretical style of some of the epistles as the only way to communicate. Doctrine, in the twentieth century, should be expounded with comparable intellectual rigour to the Epistles of Paul – there is a greater need for this, in our wishy-washy intellectual climate, than ever before. But Jesus knew that the majority of people respond initially to images and to the loving warmth of the communicator rather than to point-to-point arguments. Contact is often made first of all through the imagination, and latterly through the intellect. Neither should be despised. A close reading of the Epistles, in fact, shows there to be less of a divide from the gospels in literary form than appears at first sight. The whole book of James, the book of Jude, the book of Revelation, many passages in Paul's writings, including the 'poetic mountain top' of the New Testament in I Corinthians 13, and so on, employ powerful imagery – miniature parables – that communicate to the heart of man, to his general humanity, as well as to his intellect.

The Bible as a Source Book

With all this in mind, it is important to have a sensible attitude towards the Bible when using it as a sourcebook for writing sketches. There is a right and a wrong kind of reverence for Scripture. The wrong kind is so attached to the text, word for word as it stands, that dramatisation is impossible. In transposing print from a page into situations involving the actions of various characters, it is inevitable that some minor changes need to be made. The right kind of reverence will take the inspired word of God and translate it into language and images that can be easily understood. If Jesus said in the first century that 'the Kingdom of Heaven is like *this*', then we need in the twentieth century to say that '*this*' is like 'this'; in other words, we create new parables that speak to our own generation. Scripture hasn't been tampered with or undermined but, on the contrary, it has been brought alive for its hearers. The heart of the message must remain the same, but it is nonetheless urgent to clarify potential obscurities and to provide a meaningful 'shell' for the 'kernel' of the Truth. To associate such an approach with de-bunking trends in liberal theology can only be based on ignorance of the principles inherent in the Bible itself, where there are many examples of re-interpretation of themes, development of ideas and clarification of God's word according to the needs of particular situations. The interpretation of the 'Day of the Lord' by different prophets is one example; Paul's commentary on Exodus 34.29–35 in II Corinthians 3.13 is another. Anyone involved in translating the Bible into a primitive language will understand the right kind of freedom that is required. A friend of ours working with the Chorote Indians in the Chaco, Argentina, came up against the problem of the absence of abstract nouns in the language. 'Peace' had to be translated by the idea of 'hearing one another', which warring tribal chiefs do when they make peace. This is one example but there are many others. God has given us imaginations which need to be used as much in dramatising the message of the Christian Gospel as in anything else. For a deeper discussion of this, Tony Thiselton's article 'Understanding God's Word Today', in *Obeying Christ in a Changing World* Vol. 1 (Fount) can be highly recommended.

OTHER INDOOR PERFORMANCES

Despite the exciting nature of street theatre and the challenging effect of drama in a church service, there is a unique power in drama presented as a recognised performance in a theatre. One could, of course, substitute halls, club rooms, coffee bars with stages, and so on, but the essential elements of a traditional theatrical setting are usually there – an audience expecting to be entertained, lighting, some sort of staging, an agreed length of performance. A neutral setting of this kind has great advantages. It is free from distraction. Actors are not dwarfed by the architecture and their voices are easily heard. There is, ideally, a feeling of warmth, relaxation and 'occasion'. Many of the problems of 'tone', as regards church worship, are no longer there. The audience has chosen to come and see a performance and their minds are prepared to react accordingly. It is wise to put on performances of this kind, assuming a group have become sufficiently competent, rather than trying to justify drama as a worthwhile activity for Christians by always slotting it into a church context.

Where sketches are concerned, an evening of theatre inevitably tends towards the 'revue' – a theatrical form which generally refers to a collection of comic sketches and songs. The sketches here have a clear message and would be inappropriate in a purely 'zany' setting of comic revue, but the format of sketches and songs is useful since it is very familiar and popular. The neutral indoor setting has the additional advantage – particularly as regards the wider audience – of being less threatening than a church building. In such contexts it is wise to avoid breaking the conventions that have been set up: any preaching should be carefully co-ordinated with the sketches and should not be a surprise to the audience, revealing the drama to be merely the sugar on a rather predictable pill. Let the drama speak for itself. If a talk is given, it should be approached with great sensitivity and relevance to the evening as a whole – relaxed but meaningful comment between sketches by a 'link-man' can sometimes be the best way of approaching communication of this kind. In general, however, you should be confident in the ability of the art form to communicate in its own terms.

SKETCHES FOR OTHER INDOOR PERFORMANCES

The Parable of the Ranch

JED, a cow-boy CHUCK, a cow-boy ANNIE, a cow-girl MARY-LOU, a cow-girl MOSES, a black servant JOSHUA, a black servant OLD TIMER, servant to the Landlord BOSS'S SON, Landlord's son

This is a cow-boy version of the parable of the vineyard. It works best of all in an indoor context but a lively performance will work on the streets. If it is used in a street theatre setting it is vital to play the action to the crowd. Good costumes are essential. The two black servants are like members of a black gospel group giving a running commentary on the sketch. The parts can be played by black or white actors (without make-up) since 'gospel' is a widely shared tradition. The sketch is really a hotch-potch of cotton-picking South, wild West, Hollywood clichés and first-century Palestine, but despite this – or perhaps because of it – it has been very popular.

MOSES and JOSHUA set the props: a card table, with whisky bottle and glasses, four chairs. As they do this, they can hum, or improvise an introduction to the characters about to come on. JED, CHUCK and MARY-LOU enter and sit down. CHUCK takes out a deck of cards.

> JED: C'mon in, Annie! (*She enters*).
> ANNIE: What's the stakes, you guys?
> CHUCK: Stakes is hunnerd an' fifty bucks.
> ANNIE: Hunnerd an' fifty bucks!
> JED: 's right.
> ANNIE: Aw.
> CHUCK: I'll stand yer, Annie.
> MARY-LOU: Yeah, he's rollin' in it, ain't yer Chuck?
> JED: Not only rollin' in it, he's jumpin' in it, sleepin' in it, eatin' in it an' divin' in it.

(*Moses and Joshua comment from either
side of the stage, where they have been
sitting:*)

MOSES: But he don't own a dime of it –

JOSHUA: 'cos it all belong to de Big Boss.

CHUCK: Quit rumblin' over there!

ANNIE: Yeah, move on Moses!

MOSES: An' one of dese days de Big Boss is
gonna come right back.

JOSHUA: Amen, brother.

MOSES: Hallelujah.

JOSHUA: Prez de Lawd.

MOSES: Amen.

ALL: Shut it!

MOSES ⎫
JOSHUA ⎭ : **HALLELUJAH!**

ALL: **SHUT IT!**

MOSES ⎫
JOSHUA ⎭ : (*Softly*). Hallelujah.

MARY-LOU: Say Chuck, are all these ranch lands,
those cattle, an' them horses really
yours?

JED: He kinda borrowed 'em.

CHUCK: Permanently. (*He laughs*).

ANNIE: You sure the Big Boss ain't gonna want
them back?

CHUCK: I's sure he ain't gonna get 'em back,
Annie.

ANNIE: My! Chuck Chuckitaway, you're a real –

MOSES: Fool.

CHUCK: Hey, Annie, I'm no fool.

ANNIE: I said 'man', Chuck, 'man'.

CHUCK: Oh – gee, thanks Annie, you're a real
man too. I mean . . .

MOSES: Like I told you, he's a fool.

JOSHUA: Yeah, 'cos here comes de man from de
Big Boss, an' he's gonna be askin'
some awkward questions, man.
(OLD-TIMER *enters from behind the cow-
boys. He carries a note-book and pencil.*)

JED: Hey Chuck, the man from the Big Boss!

CHUCK: I don't see no man from the Big Boss!

OLD-TIMER: I's right behind yer.

JED
GIRLS }: (*Panic-stricken*) Let's go!

MOSES
JOSHUA }: Prez de Lawd!

CHUCK: Hold it, hold it! I ain't scared of no man from the Big Boss.

OLD-TIMER: Howdy fellers.

CHUCK: (*Long pause. Chewing*). Howdy.

OLD-TIMER: Jus' came to do a bitta stocktakin'.

CHUCK: There ain't no stock to take around here.

OLD-TIMER: Why not?

CHUCK: 'cos I just took it all.

OLD-TIMER: Boss ain't gonna like that . . . (*nervously*) fellers . . . he jus' ain't gonna be turned on by that kind of behaviour . . . (*more nervously*) fellers . . . Now he may be away on business but he's reckonin' on comin' right back. (*Long pause*) If you ask me.

JED: We *ain't* askin' yer, grand-pa.

OLD-TIMER: Well I don't care if you's askin' me or if you's ain't, I's tellin' yer. The Boss ain't gonna like this.

MOSES: No, de Boss ain't gonna like dis!

CHUCK: Maybe the Boss ain't gonna hear about it. (*They shoot him out of town.*)

OLD-TIMER: (*As he runs for it*). The Boss ain't gonna like this, fellers. (*Exit.*)

MOSES: I don't like dis. I don't like dis at all.

JOSHUA: Not one bit. Reckon de only person dey'll listen to now is de Boss's son.

MOSES: Why! Here he comes now.

MOSES
JOSHUA }: Prez de Lawd!

(*The* BOSS'S SON *walks slowly from the back of the audience and stops, facing the action.*)

MARY-LOU: Say Chuck, who's that guy?

CHUCK: Why, Mary-Lou, I don't rightly know.

ANNIE: Looks kinda smart.

MARY-LOU: Yeah, why don't yer call him over?

JED: Not so fast. I reckon I recognise that guy's eyes.

ANNIE: (*Terrified*). It's the Boss's son!

CHUCK: Yeah. *I* reckon I recognise that guy's eyes!

MARY-LOU: Watcha gonna do now, Chuck?

CHUCK: I don't know. I just . . . don't know.

ANNIE: You're a real man, eh, Chuck?

CHUCK: (*Slaps her*). Shut it!

JED: You can't mess him around, Chuck, he ain't no *ordinary* man.

MOSES: Amen?!

CHUCK: Shut it!

MOSES ⎱
JOSHUA ⎰ : Hallelujah!

CHUCK: SHUT IT!

MOSES ⎱
JOSHUA ⎰ : (*Softly*). Prez de Lawd.

ANNIE: An' I thought you were a real man, Chuck Chuckitaway.

CHUCK: C'mon Jed.

JED: I ain't layin' a finger on 'im. (CHUCK *turns his gun on* JED). I'm layin' a finger on 'im.

CHUCK: We're in this together. (*Pointing with his gun*) Annie? Mary-Lou?

ANNIE ⎱
MARY-LOU ⎰ : Uh-huh.

CHUCK: It's an old trick.

JED: But it might just work.
(*They hold out their hands in friendship to the* BOSS'S SON, *who has been standing there quietly. He walks towards them. As he holds out his right hand* CHUCK *grabs it. The two men beat him up, the girls standing guard with the guns. Finally, they twist him round to face the audience and crucify him, either on an imaginary cross or, if there is a set,*

*against some wooden stakes. Suddenly
horrified at what they have done, they
run for it. The two servants kneel for a
moment and then take him down from the
cross in slow motion. One of them carries
the body over his shoulder and they go
out singing a spiritual softly.)*

Keep On Keeping On

HEROD, a dissolute king SALOME, his step-daughter JOHN, John the Baptist, a prophet

Although this sketch is written as an encounter between John the Baptist and Herod it caricatures a familiar attitude to God, a kind of patronising interest. It can be a good talking point for a preacher or a good piece to come after a serious sketch in an indoor performance but is normally too static to work on the streets.

Herod's palace. Music. Salome dances. Herod beckons to her and she sits on his knee. Generally compromising behaviour. All through this John is watching, but they don't see him. Suddenly:

HEROD: Ha, ha! Hello John (*disentangling himself*). I was just going off to . . . er . . . do a spot of Bible study, actually. Look, could you pop back about tea-time, 4.30 suit you? And, er, (*patronisingly*) if you do pop back, take that awful thing off, will you?

JOHN: Herod, why does God make you feel uncomfortable? Why are you always running away?

HEROD: Uncomfortable with God? I wouldn't have put it that way, John, no, I've got a lot of time for God. Like him. Jolly nice chap. See him as often as I can, down at the temple. Nice place he's got there . . .

JOHN: Stop mucking around Herod. You know what the trouble with you is? You like hearing about God but you don't like listening to him.

HEROD: God's okay as far as he goes, as long as he doesn't go too far. (*Pause*) Look, John, (*embarrassed laugh*) . . . chappie.

We're men of the world, aren't we?
You and I, the two of us, together, us
two, couple of guys, ordinary chaps,
(*laugh*) you and me. You in your stuff,
all these locusts, camelskins, doing your
own thing, baptising people and all
that. John. (*Pause*) Look John, take a
tip from me, old chap. Don't overdo it.
You see, some people get bees in their
bonnets and, I mean, you don't half go
on, don't you? If we're being honest,
John . . .

JOHN: You're just a big sham.

HEROD: Oh, I'm going to have to quarrel with
you about that one, John, I mean—

JOHN: (*Ignoring him*). You have the nerve to
talk about snap visits to the temple –
the house of God. One day, sooner
than you think, you will have to meet
God face to face and then what will
you say?

HEROD: Look John, we've all slipped up here
and there, once in a while . . . more or
less. But you don't want to keep on
about sin, old man. I mean . . . none of
us is perfect, John.

JOHN: Exactly.
(*Long pause*)

HEROD: John, I'm not going to waste my time
arguing with you, old fellow. (*Seeing
Salome in the wings.*) Time's getting on,
old boy.

JOHN: That's just about it, Herod. Time's
getting on.
(*Salome beckons invitingly.*)

HEROD: Yes, well, erm, yes . . .

JOHN: There's still time to start again, Herod.

HEROD: Yes, well keep on keeping on, old man,
and don't take life too seriously. I
mean, one doesn't want to go round
losing one's head over these things . . .
(*Exit*)

Love and Death

PRISONERS LOVE DEATH

Anyone who has seen mediaeval drama, or who has read the Pilgrim's Progress, will be familiar with personifications of virtues and vices. This kind of allegorical literature has often expressed simple truths with immense power: ideas that seemed remote and 'theological' are conveyed in terms of the human drama, good and evil are shown to be more than abstract ideas, but forces conditioning our lives. Ultimately, good and evil (or here, Love and Death) can be identified with Christ and the Devil. The fight beween the two, reaching its climax at the crucifixion and resurrection, is aptly conveyed physically – violent physical struggle prevails in T.V. and film drama and, although it is severely over-emphasised, it can be shown that 'the fight' is not irrelevant to the drama of salvation (although the weapon of Christ over the Devil – uniquely – was sacrificial love). One other thing should be said about the implications of the sketch. It was a deliberate attempt to move away from passive representations of Christ, which often appear weak, to the picture of an active champion of the human cause.

Appropriate symbolic costumes should be made for LOVE and DEATH: this could be a red and white shirt emblazoned with a cross, with matching trousers in red or white for LOVE and a grey or black costume for DEATH, who has a large key hanging from his belt and also carries a trident (it should not be made from real metal). The prisoners, ragged and filthy, appear to have been enslaved for years. They are bound together by a chain. They can make their way through the audience, or from the wings, shuffling laboriously to the stage, where they collapse exhausted. DEATH enters and moves towards a large leather armchair. He snaps his fingers and the prisoners rise up. He nods with satisfaction, snapping his fingers and letting them fall. He sits down, assuming the relaxed manner of a television compere. A microphone and

P.A. can increase the intimacy of the sketch in a large building. Long speeches, such as this one, can become too static and if this is a danger cuts should be made, or DEATH should move around.

DEATH: Good evening. My name is Death. Hello. It isn't so surprising really, when you think about it – we do have to make our acquaintance sometime, sooner or later. (*Pause*) Do you find me shocking? Or perhaps it's my shadow that's most disturbing, isn't it? So they say. Well, here I am. THE LAST ENEMY! (*He gives a fake, melodramatic leer, then suddenly resumes his impassive expression. He laughs to himself.*) It's very overdone, you know, all that melodramatic stuff about bones and skulls and churchyards, creaking lids, dust collecting everywhere. I am the most predictable, normal person in the world. Superbly commonplace. So why can't people just turn round and face me? I'm here all the time you see. There's no one else, nothing beyond me, which may be a disappointment for some. I mean, all this talk about salvation, making the grade, having done enough to scrape through into heaven, to sneak in just as the door's closing . . . it's all rubbish, you know, all rubbish. No one makes the grade. It's impossible. You see . . . sin, even the smallest amount, chains you to death. To me. It's as simple as that, a simple equation, to which I hold the key. (*He holds up his key*) That's my job. I take everything, everyone. (*Pointing to individual prisoners, who raise their heads and look out to the audience despairingly*). Look at her, she used to have faith that God was looking after everything. But then her two-year old son drowned in a fish pond. That took it, that took her faith. He prayed fervently about his father's bone cancer – until his father died, then he stopped praying. Perhaps God's dead as well? That girl's fiancé was killed on his motor bike a month before their wedding. I take everything, even love. (*LOVE enters.*)

LOVE: That's a lie! Love endures everything, even death. There is no end to Love.

DEATH: And that is a very foolish thing to say in my presence. Who are you?

LOVE: My name is Love.

DEATH: Meet Death.

LOVE: I know you. I have come for the key to release the prisoners. (*Death laughs silently*)

DEATH: You have no power over the key. The power belongs to the strongest. And I will destroy you, as I have always destroyed you.

LOVE: But you have never met me in the flesh before. When the perfect comes, the imperfect passes away. Perfect love removes all fear of death.

DEATH: Death is a fact, not a fear. You deal with emotions, I deal with facts. Face the facts.

LOVE: There is one fact you have overlooked: God is Love.

DEATH: Where is God here? Where is God for these people? The warmth of his love is too far away for them to feel.

LOVE: Is it? Give me the key.

DEATH: So you're prepared to die for it, are you? Very well (*holding out the key, then snatching it away*), but no one is stronger than Death.

(LOVE *and* DEATH *fight. This should be a carefully and realistically arranged stage fight. A drum may be a helpful backing.*

*During the fight, LOVE, unseen by the
audience, takes the key from DEATH's
belt. The fight ends with DEATH finding
his trident and forcing LOVE back,
finally impaling him – so LOVE hangs
crucified. DEATH turns in triumph towards
the prisoners, shouting:)*
You see? You see? I take everything.
I take everything. EVERYTHING!
*(But he suddenly discovers the loss of
the key.)*
My key . . .
*(He frantically searches the area of the
struggle, but then sees the prisoners
staring at the key, hanging from LOVE's
right hand.)*
What are you staring at?
*(Realising, he falls back with a cry.
LOVE descends from the cross, holding the
key. He unlocks the chains of the
prisoners, each one making his escape.
This should be done with plausibility –
a prisoner who has been bound for
decades, living in darkness, does not rush
from the stage, flailing his arms and
shouting for joy. His exit is slow,
mystified, amazed, his eyes hurting in the
light but his body soothed by the
experience of freedom. Each prisoner
tentatively takes his first steps towards
a new life, until only one is left. He has
turned away from love, drawing his chains
around himself.)*

LOVE: Welcome. Won't you come to the feast
as well?
PRISONER: No.
LOVE: Why not?
PRISONER: I am in chains. I deserve my sentence.
LOVE: But I hold the keys of Death and Hell.
If I make you free, you will always be
free. Don't you know who I am? *(The
prisoner shakes his head dejectedly.)*

I am Love.

PRISONER: But I have rejected Love.

LOVE: Do you really want to stay with Death?

PRISONER: No.

(LOVE *unlocks his chains gently. They
leave. The solitary figure of* DEATH
*crawls over to the discarded chains,
picks them up and gives a cry of despair.
He has been robbed of his kingdom.
Hugging the chains to himself, he
collapses.*)

Wisdom and Folly

NARRATOR WISE MAN FOOL

Certain parts of the Bible lend themselves to dramatisation very easily – this is particularly true of the wisdom literature, which contains so many powerful images. A theme can be chosen and then collated from various verses to make a script (here, the subject of wisdom and folly) or elaborated on (see the treatment of flattery in SNAKES AND LADDERS). There is no more universal image in the theatre than the fool and the following sketch has proved very reliable in performance because of its strong combination of Biblical imagery with recognisable theatrical tradition (mime and slapstick in particular). Once again, the stage directions only suggest the basic idea – the rest is up to you.

The stage is bare except for a small wooden bench. The WISE MAN, *dressed in black and wearing a bowler hat, enters. He sits on one end of the bench, facing away from the audience. Simultaneously, the* FOOL, *who wears a spotted jump-suit, a red nose and a bowler hat, enters and sits on the other end of the bench, also facing away from the audience.*

NARRATOR: Consider wisdom.
　　　　　(*The* WISE MAN *gets up from the bench
　　　　　and turns to face the audience. No longer
　　　　　equally balanced, the bench springs up
　　　　　and the* FOOL *falls onto the floor.*)
　　　　　And folly.
　　　　　Wisdom excels folly as light excels
　　　　　darkness.
　　　　　(*The* WISE MAN *walks over to the* FOOL,
　　　　　*places a foot on his chest, and turns to
　　　　　the audience.*)
　　　　　The wise man has his eyes in his head.
　　　　　(*The* WISE MAN *walks forward confidently.*)
　　　　　But the fool walks in darkness.
　　　　　(*The* FOOL *gropes along blindly.*)
　　　　　Yet I perceive that one fate comes to

both of them.
(*They collapse.*)
Then I said to myself:
(*The* WISE MAN *raises his head thoughtfully.*)
What befalls the fool, happens to me also.
Why then have I bothered to be so very
wise?
(*He collapses again.*)
For of the wise man, as of the fool,
there is no lasting remembrance –
(*They get up, approaching each other as
if they were old friends meeting in the
street, but suddenly realise their mistake.
They walk on embarrassed.*)
Seeing that in the days to come all will
have been forgotten.
The wise man dies just like the fool.
(*The* FOOL *twitches in a particular way
and dies. The* WISE MAN *copies him
exactly.*)
But consider:
(*They get up.*)
The way of a fool is right in his own
eyes.
(*The* FOOL *walks along jauntily and
bangs his head against a brick wall.*)
But a wise man listens to advice.
(*The* WISE MAN *approaches the same
brick wall, but 'hears' advice off stage
and changes direction.*)
A fool trusts in his own mind; he takes
pleasure only in expressing his own
opinion.
(*The* FOOL *talks pompously and
meaninglessly.*)
But he who walks along the path of
wisdom will be saved from his own
mind.
(*The* WISE MAN *walks on steadily,
oblivious of the* FOOL.)
The vexation of a fool is known at once

(*The* FOOL *stubs his toe and hops around the stage, screaming with agony.*)
But a wise man quietly holds it back.
(*The* WISE MAN *stubs his toe, but suppresses his feelings manfully. Despite the pain, he manages a rather contrived, nonchalant smile.*)
For even a fool who keeps silent is considered wise. When he closes his lips, he is deemed intelligent.
(*The* WISE MAN *attempts to close the* FOOL'*s mouth, but it drops open again.*)
Do not speak in the hearing of a fool for he will despise the wisdom of your words.
(*The* WISE MAN *begins to speak to the audience, but he suddenly becomes aware of the* FOOL *mimicking him from behind. He turns round. The* FOOL *immediately pretends he was looking for something, and sheepishly walks off.*)
On the lips of him who has understanding, wisdom is found.
(*The* WISE MAN *proclaims his words of wisdom with his hands, spreading outwards from his mouth, rippling like waves. The* FOOL'*s head nods up and down as he follows the motion idiotically.*)
But a rod is for the back of him who lacks sense.
(*The* WISE MAN *brings first his left hand, then his right hand down against his side. The* FOOL *hears the blows and feels the pain. Bewildered, he looks round for his attacker.*)

The following section, since it does not distinguish between the WISE MAN *and the* FOOL, *can be cut and the mime can continue with 'but tell me, where is true wisdom to be found?' However, this particular section can be very relevant to certain audiences, as well as being good fun in stage terms:*

It is *common* sense that tells us who it is
who gets bruises without knowing why.
(*The* FOOL *looks for something under the
bench, but gives himself a black eye in
doing so.*)
And has bloodshot eyes.
(*The* WISE MAN *looks at the audience
blearily.*)
Those who linger late over their wine,
gulping it down, the strong red wine.
(*The* FOOL *and the* WISE MAN *sit on the
floor, leaning their elbows on the bench,
and drink copiously.*)
In the end it will bite like a snake and
sting like a cobra.
(*Suddenly their hands become snakes
attacking them.*)
Then your eyes see strange sights.
(*The* FOOL *rolls up one of the* WISE MAN'*s
trouser legs and stares at his leg,
horrified.*)
Your wits and speech are confused.
(*The* WISE MAN *mutters incoherently, and
his elbow slips off the bench, causing him
to lurch forward.*)
You become like a man tossing out at
sea, clinging to the top of the rigging.
(*They both get up and stand on the
bench unsteadily. They grip each other's
hands, as if holding onto the rigging, and
sway backwards and forwards.*)
You say 'if it lays me out, what do I
care?
If it brings me to the ground, what of it?
(*They let go to shrug their shoulders and
in doing so, fall off the bench.*)
As soon as I wake up, I need another
drink.
(*They prop themselves up and swing
their right arms round for another drink.*)
But tell me, where is true wisdom to be
found?

(They both stand up and walk forward.)
Not in knowledge, certainly.
For knowledge merely fosters pride.
(The FOOL *poses as an arrogant
professor.)*
But wisdom sees things as they really
are.
(The WISE MAN *bends down and picks a
'dandelion clock' which he blows,
watching the seeds float away on their
parachutes.)*
What's the use of a fool who has
money in his hand to buy wisdom,
when he has no mind to put it in?
(The WISE MAN *looks under the* FOOL's
*hat to see if he has a mind, but shakes
his head sadly.)*
One man pretends to be rich.
(The FOOL *produces a wodge of notes
and smokes a cigar.)*
Yet has nothing.
(Suddenly the FOOL *becomes poverty-
stricken.)*
Another pretends to be poor.
(The WISE MAN *hugs himself like a
freezing beggar.)*
Yet has great wealth.
(He discovers that all the world is his.)
But when we have thought all our
thoughts, spoken all our words, asked
all our questions and planned all our
answers, where shall wisdom be found?
Where is the source of understanding?
(During this the FOOL *has searched vainly
for wisdom. He looks under the bench,
bangs the top of his hat, shakes it out,
checks his pockets. He sits down on the
bench and stares at his shoes hopelessly
during the following sequence.)*
It is hidden from the eyes of all
creatures.
(The WISE MAN *bends down, as if*

concealing something in his hands.)
And concealed from the birds of the air.
(*Linking his hands together like wings,
he watches them flutter up and fly into
the sky*.)
Death says: 'I have heard a rumour of
it.'
(*He whispers the rumour from behind
his hand*.)
Pardon?
(*He listens, hoping to catch it*.)
God, who looks to the ends of the
earth and sees everything under
heaven, understands the way to it.
He saw wisdom, declared it, established
it and searched it out.
(*He scans the earth slowly, from West
to East and from North to South*.)
Thus, the fear of God is the beginning
of wisdom.
(*He takes his hat off and kneels*.)
To depart from evil is understanding.
(*He pushes evil to the right and the left
and stands*.)
God looks from Heaven upon all people
to see if there are any that are wise and
seek after God.
(*He points with his outstretched arm
slowly round the audience*.)
He has put eternity into the mind of a
man, yet no full comprehension from
beginning to end.
(*He raises his arms from his sides slowly
and majestically, bringing his left arm
vertically above his head but his right
arm short by forty five degrees –
forming an incomplete circle*.)
For God is greater than the mind of a
man.
(*He moves his hands down, as if
descending a ladder, until he is kneeling
once more*.)

The fool says in his heart:
(*The* FOOL *gets up and walks forward,*
with the thumbs and forefingers of his
hands joined together into a heart shape
against his chest.)
'There is no God.'
(*The* FOOL *lifts up the 'heart' to look*
through its emptiness at the audience. He
lowers it onto his chest again. His
mouth open, he stares into space.)

Snakes and Ladders

SON FATHER LOOSE WOMAN, a party goer DOG-OWNER, a
patronising superior at work BALLOON-BLOWER, a malicious
friend OTHER ACTORS FOR THE GROUP MIME, optional – if
used, they should be directed carefully.

*This text is printed without specific stage directions as an
encouragement to experiment. It was first performed on Thames
Television as a monologue. The actor was dressed as a harlequin and the set consisted of a gigantic snakes and ladders
board, with a huge dice used as a seat. At the end of the sketch,
the set 'vanished' leaving the harlequin sitting on his dice as if
floating in space, thinking about flattery. Since its first performance it has been adapted for the stage and its most recent
production device has been a photographic studio. The principal
characters of the* FATHER, THE LOOSE WOMAN, THE DOG-OWNER
and the BALLOON-BLOWER *have been directed as a family
group which the photographer (the* SON) *has been trying to pose.
The introductory section of the sketch has been arranged as a
series of snap shots; then each character, in turn, has emerged
from the group to encounter the* SON *in their respective scenes.
It is probably best to adopt a similar style, or employ a group
mime which can (to choose one example) wreathe their hands
like snakes round the* FATHER *as he describes the effect of
flattery. There is nothing to stop a talented actor, however,
returning to the idea of a monologue – but he will need to
evoke all the characters clearly.*

SON: There are some people in the world
who never smile
because they are depressed, angry, too
clever, too busy
to smile.
And there are some people
who smile all the time
because they are nervous or stupid or
cunning or cruel.
But most of us prefer to strike a balance.

We smile when something is funny
when we see children playing in the park
when we are happy
when we are in love!
At other times we prefer to remain
serious
in hospital
in church
during the News at Ten.
If, however, we are to live a peaceful life,
we must learn to avoid the tricks
of those who smile too much
and among all those who smile too much
we must learn to distinguish
the smile of the flatterer.
Now when I was a little child my father
said to me:

FATHER: My son! Hear your father's instructions
and pay attention, that you may be wise.
Be careful to do everything I tell you
and you will walk on your way securely
and your foot will not stumble.
BEWARE OF FLATTERY!
The smiles of an enemy are worse
than the criticisms of a friend.
The man who laughs at your jokes
may stab you in the back.
The woman who praises your looks
may seek to destroy you.
Do not be taken in!
See how the flatterers smile and nod
and wink
and pat you on the back
and see how they place their coils
around you
with every compliment, like snakes!

SON: Now the first kind of flatterer I was
warned about was the simplest to
detect. My father said to me:

FATHER: My son! Pay attention to my advice.
The lips of a loose woman drip honey
and her speech is smoother than oil

but in the end she is as sharp as a
two-edged sword.

SON: Watch now, how she approaches!
She is like a person preparing to eat a
delicious meal.

LOOSE WOMAN: How super to see you! Everybody's been
talking about you, all over the town.
I've heard such a lot about you!

SON: Her aim is to put me on a plate of my
own self-esteem, where she can liberally
spread me with praise.

LOOSE WOMAN: I'm so excited to meet you.

SON: First, the plate.

LOOSE WOMAN: I've been longing to find out all about
you.

SON: Then, the butter.

LOOSE WOMAN: You know, I thought you were very
funny at that party last week but I
didn't have the nerve to come and speak
to you.

SON: Notice how thickly she spreads it on.

LOOSE WOMAN: I thought – he wouldn't want to come
and speak to someone like *me*.

SON: After this, she pours on the honey.

LOOSE WOMAN: You're so witty, you know – so well-
dressed – so clever at your work – so
kind of you to stop and talk to me.

SON: Finally, she sandwiches me between her
compliments and takes me home for
supper.

LOOSE WOMAN: Your hair is incredibly soft.

SON: Munch.

LOOSE WOMAN: Your shoulders are so brown.

SON: Munch.

LOOSE WOMAN: So beautiful.

SON: Munch.

LOOSE WOMAN: So delicious.

SON: MUNCH MUNCH MUNCH.
(*The* FATHER *intervenes*)

FATHER: It is not good to eat much honey
so be sparing of complimentary words.

SON: Now the second kind of flatterer I was

                warned about was harder to detect. My
                father said to me:

FATHER: Watch out for the dog-owner, who ties you
           to a leash of flattery, who praises you
           to keep you under his control!

SON: See how the dog-owner approaches,
        like a man about to tame an animal.

DOG-OWNER: I would be extremely interested to know
               your opinion.

SON: As he listens attentively to what I am
        saying, he fixes on the collar.

DOG-OWNER: Is that so? How fascinating! Of course,
               you're a great expert at this sort of thing.

SON: Then, as he nods his head to every
        suggestion I make, he fixes on the leash.

DOG-OWNER: You're absolutely right.

SON: He says.

DOG-OWNER: I couldn't agree more.

SON: He says.

DOG-OWNER: I'm so glad I came to see *you*.

SON: He says. And now he takes me for a
        walk.

DOG-OWNER: I have tremendous confidence in your
               ability. You must feel free to come and
               chat to me at any time because
               obviously you've got a lot of important
               things to say.

SON: However, the dog-owner is not the
        slightest bit interested in what I have to
        say. He is merely enjoying taking me
        for a walk and tossing me a few scraps
        now and then to keep me quiet.

DOG-OWNER: I know I can depend on you.

SON: (*Gulp*)

DOG-OWNER: If more people were like you, my job
               would be easier.

SON: (*Gulp*)

DOG-OWNER: You're just the sort of person the world
               needs.

SON: (*Gulp*)

FATHER: The man who makes his neighbour look
         small is a fool.

SON: I have always kept to my father's advice and learnt now to recognise the art of the flatterer. Now the third kind of flatterer I was warned about was even harder to detect. My father said to me:

FATHER: Look out for the double-edged remark, the praise that pumps you up and up and up. Watch out for the balloon-blower!

SON: See how this man approaches, trapping me between his teeth like the neck of a balloon.

BALLOON-BLOWER: You're doing so well.

SON: He says.

BALLOON-BLOWER: How do you do it? How do you manage to keep so calm?

SON: He begins to blow: phhhhh!

BALLOON-BLOWER: To be so clever?

SON: Phhhhh!

BALLOON-BLOWER: To be so self-assured?

SON: Phhhhh!

BALLOON-BLOWER: To handle all the problems that you handle with such incredible ease?

SON: Phhhhh!

BALLOON-BLOWER: I wish I had half the ability that you have!

SON: He says. And now he pauses for breath.

BALLOON-BLOWER: Of course, I am the last person who should criticise *you* in any way.

SON: Phhhhh! I am nearly at my fullest extent, when – of course – he can destroy me with ease. He gives one final blow.

BALLOON-BLOWER: As you know, I've always agreed with everything you've ever done.

SON: Phhhhhhhhhhhh!

BALLOON-BLOWER: But some people are saying: such and such, and such and such, and such and such.

SON: BANG! I deflate to a pathetic rag. Having thus destroyed me with his criticisms, the balloon-blower commiserates.

BALLOON-BLOWER: I don't know what they're complaining about myself.

SON: He discards the balloon.

BALLOON-BLOWER: Personally, I'd back you up all the way.

FATHER: There are friends who pretend to be friends, but under their lips is the poison of vipers.

SON: I am glad that my father warned me about flattery. He said:

FATHER: Be careful to do everything I tell you and then you will walk on your way securely and your foot will not stumble.

SON: I have kept to the ladders and avoided all the snakes, just as in the game. Of course, I have slipped up every now and then but we all do, don't we? We can't all be perfect. The main thing is to live one's life as best one can and if we do make a mistake we mustn't blame ourselves too much. No, by and large, I have lived a good, honest life – knowing when to be serious and when to smile. When to be strict and when to be gentle. When to work hard and when to relax And how to avoid flattery.

FATHER: But the hardest flattery of all to detect is in yourself.

(*Blackout*)

THINK BEFORE YOU ACT

A lot of people who have been brought up in a strict church tradition regard drama as wrong. You notice that we do not say 'Christian' tradition for the simple reason that we do not believe that genuine Christian tradition, least of all the Bible, condemns the performance of plays or sketches. But nonetheless church traditions of various kinds have opposed the theatre (justifiably in many cases, bearing in mind the corruption in theatres and acting troupes since time immemorial). This, however, is a separate issue. The nature of drama cannot be blamed for the abuses of actors, just as commerce cannot be held responsible for corrupt practices in the business world.

Anyone involved in drama should care very deeply about the questions that it raises, particularly in the minds of Christians who have been brought up with a negative attitude. These questions and answers are a simple guide to some of the issues but are by no means definitive. A full discussion requires a separate book.

Why should Christians be interested in drama?

The Bible shows that powerfully written stories, vivid pictures, parables and acted out illustrations have often been God's method of communicating to man (see *The Bible and Drama*, p. 81).

Drama is a gift from God to help us explore the world, enjoy it, to be moved by suffering, to laugh at the funny side of life, to provoke ourselves and others to thought.

Drama has become the most popular form of entertainment and communication today. Television and radio have brought drama, once an occasional form of entertainment, into the vast majority of homes on a day to day basis. It would be quite possible for a child growing up in the 'dramatised society' of the late twentieth century to spend ten years of his or her life just watching television. It would not be unusual for anyone, child or adult, to watch three hours drama a night, seven days a week, and the best part of 365 days a year.

If the church fails to come to terms with drama in our present age, it fails in its mission. No matter how glorious the worship of contemporary Christianity, the church will always fail if it does not seek to be salt and light in the world and if it does not obey Christ's command to go *out* and preach the gospel to every creature.

What about those who say that 'drama is of the devil'?

To say that 'drama is of the devil' is to misunderstand drama. It is a form of art and can be used in very many different ways. Like atomic power, for instance, drama can be used for good and for evil.

To say that 'drama is of the devil' is willingly to hand over to the devil the control of many millions of people's leisure hours, to discourage young Christians from wanting to write thoughtful plays for television and to dampen the desire of acting groups in churches to communicate God's truth with freshness.

Nonetheless, some people's experience of drama may have involved watching violence, corruption, sexual immorality, without any form of judgement passed on these negative sides of human experience. They may also have seen badly and thoughtlessly put together sketches in their church which have failed to convince them of the positive potential of drama. Those interested in drama should always respect those who are either opposed to their work or cautious in their attitude towards it; they should never be unable to take helpful criticism, even when accompanied by unhelpful criticism; always seek for the 'soft answer that turns away wrath' when differences arise inside or around a drama group; and prove by the quality and commitment of their work, rather than by arguments, that drama can play a vital part in the life of the church.

Is it right to pretend to be something you are not?

Pretence is a loaded word. It suggests hoodwinking people and spiritual danger for the actor. But acting has nothing to do with false identities and all their criminal associations. Acting is a recognised art, accepted by both audience and actor. This means an agreement by which an audience, in full knowledge that we are seeing Jack Smith, agree to regard him as a character in a play. He is not pretending to be anything (in the literal sense of 'claiming to be' that person), he is simply Jack Smith playing a part in a play. The advantage of this is that the audience can be made to see and understand things which they would not be able to if they were presented with the man as himself. He will express opinions that he does not hold but at the same time no normal audience is going to assume that he is committed to believing them personally. There is a further fear, of course, that Jack Smith himself will start to hold these opinions by 'pretending' to have them (see the next question), but a reverent examination of the Bible (and of what happens when a preacher tells an anecdote or characterises an attitude from the pulpit) leads one to assume that God does have a place for role playing of this kind. The prophets were renowned for symbolic actions and behaviour – in some cases causing them to assume attitudes that were in tension with their own personalities – and it was understood that they were doing this not to delude, but to enlighten. St. Paul seems to relate Christian witness to adopting a specialised role according to circumstances, in I Corinthians 9.19–23, summarised in the words: 'I have become all things to all men, that I might by all means save some.'

Is it right to act an evil part on stage?

Since the Christian is in communion with God he not only knows more about the nature of good in life, but also more about the nature of evil as God sees it. He sees the terrible severity of adultery, anger, dishonesty, double-mindedness;

he sees the utter wreckage that they make of our world. Therefore a primary function of drama for him is the exposure of the true nature of evil. Such an exposure may well be tough meat, but the world will never sit up and pay attention to the message of Christians who act out only positive emotions on stage. This leads eventually to a plastic replica of life without problems, and without real people; and where words or gestures concerning the judgement or love of God have absolutely no meaning whatsoever. We have moved out of theatre into the world of sentimental Christmas cards.

Having said this, the problem starts. How can a Christian act an evil part without becoming polluted in the process? And how can audiences be protected from merely relishing the sight of evil rather than reacting against it? But one might go further. How is a man to read the Bible without relishing the stories of the temptation of Eve, or David and Bath-Sheba, or Judas, or Ananias and Sapphira? The answer is that the Bible creates a clear context around these stories to help us assess them and their importance. The same should be true for Christian dramatists and actors: all actions take their meaning from the integrity of the framework in which they are set. An example of this is the character of 'Morality Slipping' in a play performed by Riding Lights. The actress is called upon to play the part of an adultress but, because of the framework of the play, her role can be seen as morally destructive. This is also true in a Breadrock sketch (not included here) about the demoniac 'Legion'. In this case the actor plays the demon-possessed man with the frightening characteristics of the modern psychopathic criminal, yet all this is to show how radical is the healing brought about by his encounter with Christ. Frameworks such as these, however, are not the only possible justification for the portrayal of evil on stage – the classic Shakespearian drama 'Macbeth' deals with the corrupting power of evil on a man's soul with greater power than would be possible in the limited context of the sketch or morality play; but the integrity of the play is guaranteed by the creation of other characters and perspectives, including the prompting voice of Macbeth's conscience. Evil is seen for what it is (the same goes for Marlowe's Faustus and many other famous plays) – dangers arise when situations are

presented so 'dispassionately' as to suggest that there is little
to choose between good and evil.

As far as Christian productions are concerned, individual
actors need to pray carefully about the parts they play and
considerable thought should be given to decorum.

'Decorum' can be defined as what is fitting in a given
situation: some things are much better treated by inference
in a church service than actually dramatized. And there may
well be scenes that are potentially true to life which the
Christian will decide not to dramatise because of the sensi-
tivities of his audience, a question of modesty for his actors,
or a genuine doubt as to whether anything positive can be
achieved.

As far as an actor 'becoming like his evil character' is
concerned, this is not really the danger. What he will discover – on the contrary – is that there are many aspects of
his personality and thought-life which identify with the part
he is playing but which belong to him and are nothing to do
with a fictional creation. In recognising this evil he needs to
surround himself with prayer and forgiveness and use his
Christian perspective to give credibility to his acting.

Risks will always be involved in any kind of art. Every
production needs constant thought. There are no easy
answers available, particularly the easiest of all, which is to
avoid drama because it involves making difficult decisions.
As human beings we have to take responsibility for many
risks and decisions and drama is no exception, but those
who seek the Truth in all respects will find that their attempts
to communicate will be honoured by God.

Is it right to portray Christ?

Some people believe that to act Christ is to present a
diminished and inadequate picture of God and therefore to
encourage false worship. They might approve of the film
Ben Hur, where the face of Christ is never seen, but not of
the naturalistic portrayal in the film *Jesus of Nazareth.*
Obviously no human actor can give an accurate picture of
Christ and it may be best to avoid it if there is any danger of
belittling the majesty of God or of twisting the truth of the
gospel.

In *Jesus of Nazareth* four hundred million people saw a vivid dramatisation of the gospel story all round the world, many of them for the first time and in most cases people who would never have turned to the written accounts. It would have been impossible, and pedantic, to attempt to dramatise the gospel without an actor playing Christ. And it is unlikely that those people whose caution would prevent them from portraying Christ in drama could have achieved anything like the level of this communication by sermon or by literature. This is not an answer to the problem, it merely highlights the difficulty: to portray Christ involves the risk of some distortion, but not to portray him at all risks encouraging widespread ignorance of the gospel story.

Jesus of Nazareth is an example of Christ played naturalistically but in most sketches including the figure of Christ we have chosen a symbolic or allegorical approach. Stylisation can work like a simple pointer to a profound truth and people can rapidly pass from the limitations of the actor to consideration of a greater truth.

There is another point to make in what is really a discussion beyond the scope of this book. Our reluctance to portray Christ, although an indication of reverence, can also be a reluctance to face up to the incarnation. Jesus did take human form and it can be helpful to remind ourselves of how approachable he was in a physical sense, and how like ourselves, through the instance of a fellow human being acting the part on stage.

Isn't it all just a 'gimmick'?

Some fear that the arts, particularly the performing arts, are a 'gimmick' for Christians seeking emotive techniques for preaching the Gospel. There is no doubt that, in the age of salesmanship-technique in evangelism and even more sinister commercial exploitation of Christianity, this is a potent danger. Heretical sects are notorious for winning men's allegiance with every kind of soft-soap technique and often exploit the arts as part of this brainwashing process. It is equally possible for misguided Christians to 'use' art in this way, letting it become a tool for their systems rather than a natural fruit of a healthy church community. A common response to this danger is to outlaw gifts that are pure in themselves: it becomes a point of piety to give people the 'unadorned Gospel', the 'straight Truth', 'old-time religion'. Humour and frequent use of analogies and stories by preachers begin to become suspect. Certainly, specific artistic work in church is seen as a 'cancer' creeping in to lead the serious-minded Christian away from his lawful preoccupation with Truth.

This austerity is appealing in a day when the saccharine world of show-business invades our private lives through television, coating human relationships with superficiality and cheap glitter. We are invited daily to bow to the idols of materialism and success, and so the Christian who stands out against this fulfils a vital ministry. The truth is, *all* Christians should stand out against this and those involved in the arts, most vigorously of all. It is quite wrong to make a false opposition between 'art-less' preachers of the word and 'arty' Christians employing emotive techniques. A proper understanding of God's word shows that art is an essential aspect of man's spiritual existence: indeed, in a world dominated by materialistic philosophies, it is one of the evidences for it. (See the article: 'The Bible and Drama'.) John Calvin, sometimes erroneously quoted as the 'patron saint' of artless Christianity, said: 'All the arts come from God and are to be respected as divine inventions.' Calvin's strictures were rightly aimed at the arts in the context of idolatry, and such temptations to false worship are prevalent today, but it bears constant repetition that the misuse of the arts is one thing, intrinsic suspicion of art is another. On one notable occasion, in 1546, Calvin gave his support to the performance of a miracle play on the Acts of the Apostles, in Geneva, and later dismissed the criticism of another Christian who had mounted a fierce attack on the production. The Puritan Divines of the seventeenth century, for all their righteous indignation (frequently justified) levelled at idolatrous art, have never been excelled in the fluency of their prose or the brilliance of their metaphors in expounding the Christian Gospel. Before a misconceived notion of 'old-time religion' is brought to bear against Christians offering artistic gifts to God, the context of our predecessors' words and actions should be examined carefully and their own creativity recognised.

With all this in mind, it is dangerous for Christians to enthuse about the arts wholly in the context of church services, as if they offered the only 'spiritual justification', and so Sunday services become a kind of holy television set for believers. Sketches such as these, plays for the theatre, concerts, dances and other art forms should be allowed to develop in their own right. Church worship and evangelism can be influenced naturally and rightly by the offering of artistic gifts without becoming a jamboree. At the same time, productions in other contexts, outside 'religious' settings, can honour God provided Christians are employing their artistic talents with integrity.

GOD AND HUMOUR

Most people enjoy a good joke. Happy and abundant laughter is one of the most precious gifts that mankind has been blessed with by the Creator, who made man 'in his image'. Because of this, laughter on earth can be seen as a reflection of the laughter and joy which ring out eternally in Heaven. Of all literary forms comedy, with its inference of a happy ending giving meaning to all the disasters along the way, best portrays a truly Christian perspective on life. Dante's famous epic poem about the pilgrimage of a Christian soul was felicitously called 'the Divine Comedy'. God has promised his people full redemption from sin and death and given to us a joyous hope of the eternal 'happy ending' in Heaven.

Christian joy is not just naïve escapism but is firmly based on the promise of God, and the promise is not just reserved for the future. James begins his letter by exhorting his brethren to 'count it all joy ... when you meet various trials' (James 1 v. 2) and Paul was constantly saying things like 'Rejoice in the Lord always; again I will say, rejoice' (Phil. 4 v. 4). This kind of joy should run deep, right to the core of our being. Although humour and its effect, laughter, cannot possibly express the totality of our joy, they are important evidence of this deeper spiritual reality. When the Israelites are brought back to their own land from exile in Babylon the psalmist describes the reaction of the people to the Lord's blessing: 'Then our mouth was filled with laughter and our tongue with shouts of joy' (Psalm 126).

There is clearly some distinction between the exultant laughter that bubbles up as a result of redemption and the equally God-given laughter of 'seeing the funny side of life', but as human experiences they are close cousins. What is strange is that Christians have often been afraid of laughter being connected in any way with preaching the message of redemption. If the message itself produces joyous laughter then it is appropriate that humour and laughter should sometimes be involved in the telling of it. This is not, in any sense, to undermine the message by mockery but rather to accompany it with humorous illustration as a means of relaxed communication. One of the greatest English preachers, C. H. Spurgeon, was renowned for the way he often used humour in his sermons; it was in his nature to do so and was in no way contradictory to the gospel he preached. One could go further and say that if humour has a right place within Christian experience then it should be there as an 'enrichment' of life, and it is important that the 'riches' of the Christian life should be evident to others. Someone has remarked: 'The reason why there aren't more people going into church may well be the looks on the faces of those going out.' Of all people, Christians should be people who can be happy, who can laugh, enjoy the fun of living and even laugh at themselves from time to time.

The Educational Value of Humour

As the different cycles of mystery plays developed, realism and humour were progressively introduced. As one might expect, this process began with the lowest characters in the overall hierarchy (the Devil, Herod, Pilate, Noah's unmanageable wife, the Shepherds and the rogue, Mak the Sheep Stealer, the soldiers at the cross) but gradually came to influence the conception of many other characters. As well as increasing the enjoyment for the spectator and commanding his attention and responsiveness more closely, this humorous realism was fulfilling a 'homiletic' purpose, namely to teach and warn people about the undignified and foolish ways of men. The book of Proverbs uses many comic touches for a similar purpose. The image of the sluggard, for instance, turning over in his bed 'like a door turns on its hinges' is meant to be funny and any dramatisation of that verse would also be funny. Far from diluting the force of the message, the humour in this case strengthens our understanding of the folly of sloth. In this way, satire which has a positive intention is a very useful tool for the Christian artist. Satire can be cruel and destructive, however, even in Christian hands (some of the more extreme writings of the eighteenth-century author, Jonathan Swift, demonstrate this). As an artistic device it needs careful control.

Remember that, in literary terms, humour and its uses have been comparatively recent developments. It would be wrong to expect to find in the Bible, for example, an extended treatment of a comic theme, just as it would be wrong to expect to find a detailed discussion of the nature of physics. In English literary tradition there has always been a strong ingredient of comedy which has gradually changed as various types of humour have gone in and out of fashion. The figure of the 'Fool' or court jester in Shakespearian drama is one example, for here the figure of fun (as opposed to the 'Fool' in 'Wisdom and Folly') is also the voice of wisdom. The humorist is as memorable for his perception about human existence as for his witticisms. The 'Fool' in 'King Lear', for all his buffoonery, is the only member of the court who is allowed to tell the king the truth. He does not flinch from his task, but he expresses himself in such a way as to call forth laughter as well as sorrow, and the truth is made easier to accept.

The Profound Implications of Humour

It is just this very issue of the interplay between truth and humour that has helped one eminent sociologist nearer to faith in God in recent years. In his book, *A Rumour of Angels*, Peter Berger analyses, amongst other things, the religious significance of humour. In essence, he argues as follows: anything that is comic depends upon a basic discrepancy or incongruity in order to be funny. This relates entirely to human situations (animals, for instance, are only comic when we view them as having human characteristics). The fundamental discrepancy from which all other discrepancies are derived is the discrepancy between man and the universe. The world is full of suffering, evil and death within which the human spirit is imprisoned. An appreciation of the comic puts this discrepancy into its right perspective and by laughing at the imprisonment of the human spirit, humour implies that the imprisonment is not final but will be overcome. This is quite different from many contemporary artists' and writers' notion of 'absurd laughter' in the face of a futile predicament. Humour, in this interpretation, is an intimation of redemption and can be seen as an ultimately religious vindication of joy. Such laughter points beyond the (often appalling) limits of the empirical world to the Divine ordering and love of God.

Humour and the Christian Sketch-Writer

From the profundity of philosophical arguments one needs to come back to earth and consider more precisely the advantages that humour can have for the sketch-writer, and in particular the Christian sketch-writer. Firstly: entertainment. Every theatrical performance, *by its very nature*, involves elements of entertainment. With the predominance of television and films today man lives surrounded by entertainment and Christians need to learn the art in order to communicate. Jesus himself was a great entertainer ('he never spoke without a parable') and understood the importance of using this to capture people's attention. Laughter helps an audience to relax and register their involvement in the performance. A sketch can be weakened by too much self-indulgent humour, but if the main point of a sketch is always kept in view various ingredients of entertainment along the way will assist in its communication. Jesus, very deliberately, described himself as a bridegroom at a wedding and, while the business of marriage is serious, the atmosphere at any Jewish wedding was full of festivity and enjoyment.

Secondly: we need to distinguish different types of laughter.

(1) *Sympathetic laughter:* There are many endearing things about human behaviour which are simply funny and ought to raise a laugh.

(2) *Laughter of recognition*: As an audience laughs at a caricature or a situation, they laugh because they know it to be true of themselves. The laughter has the effect of educating the audience. Sir Philip Sydney, in the sixteenth century, talked about poetry as a 'medicine of cherries', i.e. something you enjoy which also does you good, and this has a lot in common with the laughter of recognition.

(3) *Nervous laughter*: A psychological reflex to an embarrassing and maybe frightening situation. This can be the result of ineptitude on the part of the dramatist, but it can also be an indication that he is really hitting home.

(4) *Thoughtless Laughter*: The Bible calls this 'levity'. It is an idle kind of joking at something which isn't funny at all.
(5) *Mockery*: This kind of laugh intends to degrade and insult whatever is mocked. It is the verbal equivalent of spitting. Mockery also includes the laughter of disbelief.

In the story of Abraham and Sarah, the news of God's promise of a son produces in each of them a different kind of laugh, though the Hebrew word is the same. The Lord's reaction to their laughter points up the difference. Abraham laughs apparently with joy and amazement at the incongruity of aged parents having a baby, but Sarah laughs to herself in mocking disbelief, which she later tries to deny (Gen. Chs. 17, 18). As Christians we need to be sure about the motives for our laughter.

Humour at the Heart of God's Communication to Man

People quite often speak about God's sense of humour, not irreverently, but in the context of the loving and gentle way which God uses to guide and to teach us, to stop us doing certain things and to make us do others. In his wisdom and with humour God appeals to *our* sense of humour and in a helpful and loving way the laugh is on us. When God communicates to Noah in one of the mystery plays he calls him 'my darling dear'; Noah, for his part, is overwhelmed with God's loving condescension and thanks 'the Lord so dear that would vouchsafe thus low to appear to a simple knave'. Such a discrepancy is comical, but at the same time profoundly sympathetic. It is in no way out of place, therefore, to discover some of the humour implicit in the background of the gospel narratives; in fact, there is probably a lot more humour than we realise. Because of the change in fashions over two thousand years we will never know for certain exactly what was funny to people in first-century Palestine. We are left with a few vestiges of humour which still make us laugh, or at least smile. From a probably very comic situation in the carpenter's shop, Jesus teaches us through the picture of the log and the mote: two men sawing a log, which slips off the bench. One man gets off lightly with nothing more than dust in his eye, but the other is unfortunate enough to receive the full force of the whole log. What is funny is that the man with a black eye tries to help the other with his speck of dust, even though he can't see straight. There is a cartoon element, too, in the striking contrast between the two debts in the story of the unforgiving servant. And surely there is humour in the actions of the four men who are so desperate for their friend to be healed by Jesus that they remove the roof of the house and lower him gently into the room, bed and all!

Some of these lighter touches in the Bible give immediate access to the deeper truths of the Gospel message. Twentieth-century men and women can see their likenesses in the people that surrounded Jesus, just as the following incident described by a woman on British television must have echoed the experience of so many blind people healed by Christ himself: this woman had the remarkable experience of being able to see, as the result of an operation, for the first time. One can hardly begin to imagine what an incredible experience this was. Amongst other first sights of things, there was the first time she saw herself in the mirror. She explained her horror at seeing this 'thing' sticking out in the middle of her face. 'My friends must have been keeping this from me for so long, and I never knew,' she said, but was later reassured when she saw that everyone else had a nose as well as her. It is natural for the sketch-writer to see in this ripe material for dramatising the story of Bartimaeus!

A Christian playwright, Christopher Fry, has said: 'Laughter is the surest touch of creation in man.' This, along with the statement by Søren Kierkegaard a century earlier, is a fitting summary of the issues raised here: 'The religious individual has, as such, made the discovery of the comical in largest measure.'

GLOSSARY

BLOCK	To plan moves for actors.
CAST	The actors taking the parts of a play. (Vb) To select actors for parts.
CORPSE	Usually means to confuse or put off an actor, causing him to lose the thread of his part, become self-aware and laugh etc.
DIRECTOR	Usual title in the live theatre for person who casts a play, runs rehearsals and decides on staging.
DOWNSTAGE	Towards the front of the stage (this derives from the time when a rake or slope in the stage was common).
DRY	To forget lines.
FLAT	Unit of stage scenery (often made of hardboard or canvas).
FLIES	Above the stage area: the space over the proscenium arch.
FLUFF	Stumble over a line.
F.O.H.	Front of house (comprising box office area, auditorium etc.)
PLOT	Mainly used in connection with lighting: to arrange positions and cues for lights (lighting plot for a board operator).
PROPS	Stage properties – anything used by actors on stage.
SET	Stage scenery. (Vb) To put props or scenery in position.
STAGE RIGHT STAGE LEFT	Positions as seen from actor to audience.
STRIKE	To remove props at the end of a scene or to dismantle a set.
TECH RUN	Rehearsal for lighting and sound cues and any technical matters.
UPSTAGE	Towards the back of the stage. (Vb) To attract attention to yourself at another performer's expense – pushing them out of the limelight.

WARM-UP — Physical exercise to improve fitness and co-ordination, often involving fast moving games as well as 'limbering up' (see Bibliography for books of example exercises).

WINGS — The sides of the stage.

WORKSHOP — A session of group exercises and experiments in drama.

BIBLIOGRAPHY

A few books for those interested in more detailed technical help with learning the craft of acting, organising workshops or even writing a play.

Practical Books
Wilton Cole, *Sound and Sense* (Allen & Unwin).
Anna Scher and Charles Verrall, *One Hundred Plus Ideas for Drama* (Heinemann Educational).
Viola Spolin, *Improvisation Games* (Pitman).
David Ceely, *Drama Kit*.
A. Sheppard, *Mime: The Technique of Silence*.
James Clifford Turner, *Voice and Speech in the Theatre* (Pitman).
Cicely Berry, *Voice and the Actor* (Harrap).

More Theoretical Books
Constantin Stanislavski, *An Actor Prepares*.
J. L. Styan, *The Elements of Drama* (Cambridge University Press).
Pemberton-Billing and Clegg, *Teaching Drama* (Hodder and Stoughton).
Ed. Hodgson and Banham, *Drama in Education* (Pitman).